Portraits of Japan
Voicing Opinions on a Changing Society

日本を知り、そして世界を知り、
そして考える

Paul Stapleton / Atsuko Uemura

Portraits of Japan—Voicing Opinions on a Changing Society

Paul Stapleton / Atsuko Uemura

© 2017 Cengage Learning K.K.

ALL RIGHTS RESERVED. No part of this work covered by the copyright herein may be reproduced, transmitted, stored, or used in any form or by any means—graphic, electronic, or mechanical, including but not limited to photocopying, recording, scanning, digitizing, taping, Web distribution, information networks, or information storage and retrieval systems—without the prior written permission of the publisher.

Photo Credits:
Front cover: © Martin Dimitrov; p. 13: © EPA=Jiji; p. 14: (l) © inci aral/iStock/Thinkstock, (r) © andrewgenn/iStock/Thinkstock; p. 19: © AFP=Jiji; p. 20: © ikopylov/iStock/Thinkstock; pp. 22, 23: (t) © yayayoyo/iStock/Thinkstock, (b) © yayayoyo/iStock/Thinkstock; p. 25: © Jiji; p. 31: © Chris Amaral/DigitalVision/Thinkstock;
p. 32: © DAJ/Thinkstock; p. 37: © Jiji Press Photo; p. 38: © Tetsu/amanaimagesRF/Thinkstock; p. 43: © Jiji Press Photo; p. 46: © MIXA next/Thinkstock; p. 49: © Jiji; p. 55: © Jiangang Wang/Getty Images; p. 58: © DragonImages/iStock/Thinkstock; p. 61: © Rex Features/Pacific Press Service; p. 67: © Alamy/Pacific Press Service; p. 73: © Bloomberg/Getty Images; p. 79: © The Hokkaido Shimbun Press/Jiji Press Photo; p. 85: © Jiji Press Photo; p. 86: © y-studio/iStock/Thinkstock; p. 91: © Jiji; p. 94: © Stocktrek Images/Stocktrek Images/Thinkstock

For permission to use material from this textbook or product, e-mail to **eltjapan@cengage.com**

ISBN: 978-4-86312-312-0

Cengage Learning K.K.
No. 2 Funato Building 5th Floor
1-11-11 Kudankita, Chiyoda-ku
Tokyo 102-0073
Japan

Tel: 03-3511-4392
Fax: 03-3511-4391

Preface

Like all countries, Japan is evolving at a rapid rate, and while much of this change is creating challenges, many of the changes are quite positive, or bringing benefits to the whole world. Most people are aware of Japan's challenges. Its population is aging and the poverty rate is increasing. At the same time, rural Japan is having trouble sustaining its villages and towns. On the surface, it may appear that Japan is stuck in the slow lane.

However, nothing could be further from the truth. Despite the difficulties, Japan remains a dynamic society. For example, Japan is a leading exporter of culture with iconic words such as anime, manga and emoji having become part of the world's lexicon. Japan is also importing ideas from abroad which are changing views about working mothers and traditional gender roles. Now that 18-year-olds can vote, Japan's digitally savvy youth have an earlier chance to voice their opinions. With the 2020 Tokyo Olympics, Japan again has the opportunity to expose its dynamism to the world. In *Portraits of Japan*, these issues and ideas, plus a few others, will be illustrated to reveal a society ready to face its challenges.

Paul Stapleton

まえがき

2015年に日本を訪れた外国人の数は2千万人に迫り、半世紀前の50倍を超えています（日本政府観光局のデータより）。また日本を訪れなくても、今はインターネットを使って日本で起きていることを瞬時に世界中で知ることができる時代です。外国人から見た日本はどんな国なのでしょうか。日本は海外から多くの旅行者を引き寄せる魅力ある国なのでしょうか。

本書は、日本の大学で長く教鞭をとった経験を持つ香港在住のカナダ人が、現在の日本について様々な視点から書いた14編のエッセイをもとにしています。「英文から情報を得て英語の学習をする」ことを目標としていることは言うまでもありませんが、本書にはもう一つ大きな目標があります。それは「自分に問うて考える」ことです。語彙、内容把握、リスニングなどの英語の学習だけでなく、いま私たちの社会で起きていることについて知り、これから皆さんが築いていく日本がどのような国であるべきかを一緒に考えましょう。

上村　淳子

Contents

Preface / まえがき ——————————————————— 3
本書の構成と効果的な使い方 ——————————————— 6

Pre-Unit People in the Book / Reading Skill ❶❷ ——— 10

Unit 1 Japanese Cultural Invasion ————————— 13
（世界に広がる日本のポップカルチャー）

Unit 2 Emoji: From Japan to the World ——————— 19
（日本発祥の絵文字はいまや世界共通語）

Unit 3 Tokyo 2020: Chance for a New Beginning ——— 25
（2020年東京オリンピックへの期待と課題）

Unit 4 Pet Obsession ——————————————— 31
（日本人のペット依存）

Unit 5 Silver Japan ———————————————— 37
（超高齢化社会ニッポンと若者の将来への影響）

Unit 6 Changing Gender Roles —————————— 43
（日本社会における男女の立場や役割の変化）

Unit 7 Maternity Harassment —————————— 49
（マタハラ：妊婦が受ける冷遇と批判の実情）

Unit 8	**Digital Youth: The Connected Generation** — 55
	（ネット世代の若者考察）

Unit 9	**Japan's Peaceful Poor** — 61
	（格差の広がる日本社会の現状）

Unit 10	**The Idol-Making Machine** — 67
	（日本独自の「アイドル」の作られ方）

Unit 11	**Japanese Hospitality: Second to None** — 73
	（世界に誇る日本の顧客サービス）

Unit 12	**Shrinking Cities: Returning the Countryside to Nature** — 79
	（過疎化による地方自治の崩壊）

Unit 13	**Student Power: The New Youth Movement** — 85
	（学生が持つ社会への影響力とその可能性：18歳選挙権の意義）

Unit 14	**Japan in Space: Leaping to New Frontiers** — 91
	（日本の宇宙開発：実績と将来への展望）

My Opinion Note — 97

Word List — 125

本書の構成と効果的な使い方

本書は Pre-Unit と全 14 ユニットで構成され、各ユニットでは現代の日本に関する重要かつ特徴的なトピックを扱います。また、巻末には **My Opinion Note** を収録しています。本文読解と段階的なアクティビティを通して、学生の皆さんに自身の現在と未来を考える機会を提供します。

［各ユニットの基本構成とアクティビティの特徴］

1ページ目

冒頭の会話

ジパング博士、サキ、ケンタ、アビーの4名の登場人物による、ユニットのトピックに関連した会話です。「このユニットにはどんなことが書いてあるのだろう？」と、その後に続く学習への扉を開ける気持ちで読んでみましょう。

Before Reading

本文への導入として、2つのアクティビティを用意しています。

Survey on the Topic

ユニットのトピックに関連した3つの日本語の質問に Yes/No で答えます。回答は二者択一なので、迷うときは「どちらかといえば」で選んでください。日頃よく考えたことがない質問もあるでしょう。この機会に自分自身の考えや意識を調査してみましょう。

Vocabulary

本文中の覚えておきたい単語を10個選び、本文で使われているフレーズにして出題しています。青色の単語の意味を確認した上で、その用法と一緒に覚えましょう。フレーズにすることで品詞が明確になり、より記憶に残り、また本文を読むときの助けにもなるでしょう。自分で別のフレーズを作るのもよいですね。たとえば、distinctive style として distinctive を覚えれば、distinctive voice、distinctive accent のように。

2〜5ページ目

While Reading

本文を2つのパートに分けて、本文のリーディングを基本としたアクティビティに加え、発展的な学習も行います。

※各ユニットの本文で述べられている内容には、著者 Paul Stapleton 氏の個人的な見解が含まれていることをご承知おきください。

2ページ目

Part 1 本文の前半です。Unit 1〜7 では、内容に重要な意味を持つ内容語の中でも特に重要と思われるキーワードを太字にして掲載しています。Unit 8〜14 では、まとまった意味を持つフレーズの切れ目でスラッシュ（/）を入れています。

3ページ目

Exercises

(1) Unit 1〜7 では太字の語句に注意しながら本文を一読しましょう。Unit 8〜14 では、切れ目（/）ごとに意味をとり、本文を一読しましょう。英文全体の大意がつかめたら、1〜3 の英語が説明する単語を本文中から探してください。知らない単語であっても、文脈から考えて説明と合う単語を見つけましょう。辞書を引かずに知らない単語の意味を推測する練習です。

(2) Part 1 で述べられている内容を別の英文で考える問題です。別の英語表現で確認することにより、内容理解をさらに高めます。

(3) サキとケンタが Part 1 の内容に基づいて日本語で会話をしています。空所に適語を記入して会話文を完成し、Part 1 の内容をまとめてから Part 2 へと進みます。

Thinking Time!

巻末の **My Opinion Note** を使用します。Part 1 で読んだ内容をもとに、5つの質問に答えましょう。回答は Yes/No か Agree/Disagree の二者択一なので、「どちらかといえば」で選んでください。「自分に問う」時間です。

4ページ目

Part 2　本文の後半です。太字もスラッシュ（/）も入っていない状態です。

5ページ目

Exercises

(4)　Unit 1～7 では、Part 1 において太字で示されていた語句のように、内容に重要な意味を持つと思われるキーワードを自分で見つける練習です。慣れてくると自然にキーワードを意識して読めようになります。Unit 8～14 では、Part 1 においてスラッシュ（/）で区切られていたように、意味のまとまりを自分で考えて区切る練習です。慣れてくると返り読みをせず、自然に意味のまとまりで読めるようになり、英文を読むことがもっと楽になります。

(5)(6)(7)　Part 2 の英文について理解した内容をもとに解く記述問題です。日本語でまとめることで著者の論点をしっかりと把握しましょう。((7) のないユニットもあり)

Listening Comprehension

Part 1 と Part 2 を通して読んだことをもとに、ケンタとアビーが英語で会話しています。これまで読んだ内容を音声で確認しましょう。スクリプトは掲載されていませんが、すでに得た知識や情報をもとにしていますから、まったく新しい情報についての会話よりもずっと聴き取りやすいはずです。知っている語彙で、知っている内容について聴くことにより、英語の音に慣れ、リスニングに自信をつけましょう。

Thinking Time!

巻末の **My Opinion Note** を使用します。Part 1 と同様、Part 2 で読んだ内容をもとに 5 つの質問に答えましょう。再び「自分に問う」時間です。

After Reading

本文で使用されているフレーズのうち、ライティングやスピーキングに役立つものを選んで出題しています。提示されたフレーズも使いながら、本文とは異なる内容の英文を完成させましょう。さらに、完成した英文を音読し、全文を通して書き直すとより効果的に記憶に定着します。また、そのフレーズを使って別の英文を作ってみるのもよいでしょう。

巻　末

My Opinion Note　各ユニットにつき2ページで、切り取り式になっています。表面は Part 1 と Part 2 の Thinking Time! で使います。

Write Your Opinion　ユニットの学習のまとめとなるアクティビティで、巻末の **My Opinion Note** の裏面を使用します。本文の内容に関連した質問に答えて、自分の考えを自由に述べましょう。本書の副題は "Voicing Opinions on a Changing Society" です。日本社会について、あなたの意見を言葉で表してください。書く前に Part 1 と Part 2 を通して音読し、全体を通してもう一度内容を振り返るとよいでしょう。英語と日本語のどちらで書くかは担当教員の指示に従ってください。

※ **My Opinion Note** を授業中に使用するか、または課題として授業外で使用するかは、担当教員の指示に従ってください。

音声ファイルの無料ダウンロード　http://cengage.jp/elt/JapaneseFourSkills/

 のアイコンがある箇所の音声ファイルをダウンロードできます。

❶ 上記の URL にアクセスまたは QR コードをスマートフォンなどのリーダーでスキャン（➡ ❹ へ）
❷ 本書の表紙画像またはタイトル（Portraits of Japan）をクリック
❸ 本書のページで 音声ファイル ボタンをクリック
❹ 希望の番号をクリックして音声ファイルをダウンロード

Pre-Unit

People in the Book   音声を聴いて登場人物の自己紹介を完成させましょう。

Welcome to *Portraits of Japan*. I'm Dr. Zipangu and I specialize in (   ) (   ) and (   ). In this book, we've brought up (   ) (   ) on Japan. I'd like you to (   ) (   ) (   ) and (   ) (   ) (   ) on Japanese society.

Hi, I'm Saki. I'm a college student (   ) (   ) sociology. Next year, I'm going to study in the USA as an exchange student. I'll have many (   ) (   ) (   ) (   ) (   ) (   ) there, so I think (   ) (   ) (   ) more about Japan.

Hello, I'm Kenta. (   ) (   ) in mechanical engineering (   ) (   ). I'd like to learn more about our Japanese society because my dream is to (   ) (   ) (   ) for Japan. Let's read about today's Japan. It's a good chance to (   ) (   ) (   ) (   ).

I'm Abbie. I'm an exchange student from Florida in the United States. I came to Japan (   ) (   ) (   ) and I'm studying (   ) (   ) at college. I'm especially interested in manga and anime. I'd like to (   ) (   ) (   ) (   ) to my friends in America.

Reading Skill ❶

本テキストのUnit 1～7では、キーワードに注目しながら読む方法を学習します。英文の中で重要と思われる語を特に注意して読み、全体の意味を把握するのです。

次の英文では、キーワードを太字にしています。太字の語に注意しながら読み、あとの大意を表す日本文を完成させましょう。

Two words often **associated** with **modern Japanese culture** are **manga** and **anime**, both of which are having an **impact outside** of Japan. These two **art forms** have a **distinctive** style that has **gained popularity** in many parts of the world, especially France and the U.S.

【大意】
（　　　　　　　　）にしばしば（　　　　　　　　）2つの語は
（　　　　　）と（　　　　　）だ。どちらも（　　　　　　　）に
（　　　　）を与えている。これらの（　　　　　　）には（　　　　）
スタイルがあり、世界で（　　　　　　　）いる。

英文が伝える内容に大きな意味を持つ語は名詞、動詞、形容詞そして副詞です。それらのキーワードを意識しながら読むと、その英文の大意が把握しやすくなります。

Reading Skill ❷

本テキストの Unit 8〜14 では、英文をまとまった区切りで読むフレーズリーディングを学習します。英文を前から順に意味のまとまりで読み、後ろから前に返り読みしない方法です。

次の英文では、意味のまとまりを **/** で区切っています。前から順に読み、あとの日本語訳を完成させましょう。

Young people today **/** are never unconnected. **/** Mobile technology has given us phones **/** that have almost become part of our bodies. **/** Today's youth are the first generation **/** to grow up **/** in an always-connected world. **/** This is a huge difference **/** from their parent's generation. **/**

【日本語訳】
（　　　　　　　　　　）は **/** つながっていないということが決してない。**/** モバイルテクノロジーが（　　　　　　　　　　　　）**/** それはほとんど
（　　　　　　　　　　）なっている。**/** 今日の若者は（　　　　　　）だ **/**
成長する **/** 常に（　　　　　　　　　　）で。**/** これは（　　　　　　）だ **/**
（　　　　　　　）とは。**/**

さあ、ジパング博士、サキ、ケンタ、そしてアビーと今の日本について、日本で起きていることについて読み、そして考えましょう。

Unit 1

Japanese Cultural Invasion

 10年ほど前から日本の文化、特にポップカルチャーが海外で注目を集めている。

 そういえばアビー、あなたは日本のアニメやマンガが好きで日本に来たって本当？

 本当よ。子供の頃ずっとテレビで日本のアニメを見ていたの。そしてもっと日本の文化を知りたいと思うようになったのよ。

 アニメやマンガだけじゃない、他にも受け入れられている日本の文化がいろいろあるんだよ。

Before Reading
本文を読む前に、以下のタスクに取り組みましょう。

Survey on the Topic
次の1～3について、自分に当てはまるほうを○で囲みましょう。

1. 日本の文化は世界で注目されていると思う。　　　　　　　　　　　　[Yes / No]
2. 日本の文化より西洋の文化に興味がある。　　　　　　　　　　　　　[Yes / No]
3. 日本の文化をもっと海外の人に知ってもらいたいと思う。　　　　　　[Yes / No]

 ### Vocabulary
___ に適する青色の単語の意味を枠内から選び、記号で答えましょう。

1. **distinctive** style　　___スタイル
2. **gain** popularity　　人気を___
3. **significant** difference　　___違い
4. **vivid** expression　　___表情
5. **convey** emotion　　感情を___
6. cultural **export**　　文化の___
7. **traditional** culture　　___文化
8. **adorn** a plane　　飛行機を___
9. **spread** of culture　　文化の___
10. good **quality**　　良い___

| a. 伝統的な | b. 重大な | c. 得る | d. 品質 | e. 独特の |
| f. 装飾する | g. 広まり | h. 伝える | i. 生き生きとした | j. 輸出 |

While Reading

本文をパートごとに読み、あとの問題に答えましょう。

Part 1

 世界で受け入れられている日本文化といえば、まずマンガやアニメだ。日本独特のマンガやアニメの特徴について読んでみよう。

1. Two words often **associated** with **modern Japanese culture** are **manga** and **anime**, both of which are having an **impact outside** of Japan. These two **art forms** have a **distinctive** style that has **gained popularity** in many parts of the world, especially France and the U.S.

2. Although manga and anime are **similar** to **comics** and **cartoons** respectively, there are some **significant differences**. For example, the **characters** in manga have **vivid facial expressions** such as large eyes, which are important for **conveying emotions**. Anime comes from manga, but the colors, **three-dimensional views and backgrounds** are different from American cartoons. Cartoons tend to **focus on** the **action** and **plot** more than the **appearances**. Whereas comics and cartoons are generally for **children**, **interest** in manga and anime **spans all age groups**. **Recent blockbusters**, such as *Avatar*, may be showing that anime is having an **influence** on **Hollywood**.

Notes　associate with ...「…と結びつける」　be similar to ...「…に似ている」　respectively「それぞれ」
　　　　three-dimensional「立体的な、3Dの」　focus on ...「…に重点を置く、焦点を当てる」
　　　　span「…に広がる」　blockbuster「人気作品」

Exercises

（1）太字に注意して本文を読み、次の英語の説明と合う単語を探して、提示の語頭に続けて答えましょう。ただし、名詞は単数形を、動詞は原形を書きましょう。

1. the powerful influence that something has　　　　(i　　　　　　)
2. strong human feeling, such as love, hate or anger　　(e　　　　　　)
3. the way someone or something looks　　　　　　(a　　　　　　)

（2）本文の内容に合うように空所に適切な単語を記入しましょう。

1. The style of manga and anime is (　　　　　), and they have had an (　　　　　) outside of Japan.
2. The two countries where manga and anime are very (　　　　　) are (　　　　　) and the U.S.
3. Manga and anime are (　　　　　) to comics and cartoons, but they have (　　　　　) differences from them.

（3）空所を補って、本文の内容に関する次の会話を完成させましょう。

Kenta: 日本のマンガと西洋のマンガにはいろいろ違いがあるんだね。
Saki:　そうね、日本のマンガのキャラクターは目が大きくて顔の表情が ¹.＿＿＿＿＿＿ いる。これは ².＿＿＿＿＿＿ のに大事なことなのね。
Kenta: それと、西洋のアニメが重点を置くのは ³.＿＿＿＿＿＿ だ。
Saki:　それに色や ⁴.＿＿＿＿＿＿ な描き方や ⁵.＿＿＿＿＿＿ も違う。
Kenta: そんなマンガやアニメ独特の特徴があるから世界で、そしてあらゆる年齢層に受け入れられているんだね。

Thinking Time!

p.97 の **My Opinion Note** A を使って、自分の立場や意見を答えよう。

Part 2

 アニメやマンガの他に受け入れられている日本文化には、どんなものがあるのだろうか。さらに英文を読んでみよう。

3　Japan has also had other recent cultural exports. The government-sponsored Cool Japan campaign has been successful in exporting Japan's pop culture. Instead of promoting traditional Japanese culture, such as tea ceremony, the government realized promoting modern culture could help the economy. One of the biggest successes is Japan's love of cute things. Hello Kitty, the expressionless and mouthless kitten, now generates more search hits on the Internet than Mickey Mouse. While the cute cat can often be seen here and there in Europe and North America, it has become a cultural icon in much of Asia. Hello Kitty adorns a few planes for Eva Airways in Taiwan, and there are cafés or diners dedicated to the kitten in Australia, Hong Kong and Taiwan.

4　The spread of Japanese culture is not only limited to artistic creations such as manga and anime. It also concerns certain brands, one of which is "Hokkaido." Hokkaido has always had an image of being a place full of nature with fresh and clean products, but it is only recently that the image has spread abroad. When the name "Hokkaido" is attached to a restaurant or a product, such as seafood, milk products or certain vegetables, it gives people an image of freshness and good quality.

5　Finally, it now seems difficult to imagine our modern world without Japanese cultural icons, such as anime, manga and Pokémon. Surely, Japan has made the world a more interesting place.

Notes　**Cool Japan campaign**「クールジャパン・キャンペーン（日本の文化を世界に積極的に発信していこうという取り組み）」　**promote**「…を促進する、振興する」　**tea ceremony**「茶道」　**search**「検索」　**icon**「象徴」　**dedicated to ...**「…のためだけの」　**full of ...**「…でいっぱいの」　**product**「生産物」　**it is only recently that ...**「…はごく最近のことである」

Exercises

（4）本文のキーワードであると思われる語（句）に下線を引きましょう。

（5）ハローキティが世界で多くの支持を得ている具体例について、次の文を完成させましょう。

1. ミッキーマウスよりも _____。
2. ヨーロッパや北米 _____。
3. アジアの広い範囲で _____。
4. 台湾のエバー航空の _____。
5. オーストラリア、香港、台湾では _____。

（6）海外で広まる北海道ブランドについて、次のキーワードをすべて日本語にして用いて説明しましょう。

[image   fresh   clean   spread   name   good quality]

_____
_____
_____
_____

Listening Comprehension

Audio 09

ケンタとアビーのマンガやアニメに関する会話を音声で聴き、次の英文が会話の内容に合っていればT (True)、合っていなければF (False) を [　] に記入しましょう。

[　] 1. Abbie says that facial expressions in manga convey the characters' emotions.

[　] 2. Kenta wants a Hello Kitty badge on Abbie's bag.

[　] 3. Abbie says she has been to the Hello Kitty café before.

Thinking Time!

 p.97 の **My Opinion Note B** を使って、自分の立場や意見を答えよう。

After Reading

日本語に合うように英文を完成させましょう。なお、下線部に相当する表現は提示しています。

1. 多くの人が日本製品をしばしば高品質と結びつける。　　　　　[associate with . . .]

    Many people often (　　　　　) Japanese products (　　　　　) good (　　　　　).

2. クジラは外見は魚に似ているが、哺乳類だ。　　　　　[be similar to . . .]

    Whales (　　　) (　　　) (　　　) fish in (　　　), but they are mammals.

3. 私はパリに滞在中、日本の伝統に焦点を当てたテレビ番組を見た。　　　　　[focus on . . .]

    (　　　) I was (　　　) (　　　) (　　　), I saw a TV program which (　　　) (　　　) Japanese (　　　).

4. そのレストランはいつも多くの客でいっぱいだ。　　　　　[be full of . . .]

    The (　　　) (　　　) always (　　　) (　　　) lots of diners.

5. 海外で和食が人気になったのはごく最近のことだ。　　　　　[it is only recently that . . .]

    (　　　) (　　　) (　　　) (　　　) that (　　　) (　　　) has gained (　　　) outside of Japan.

Unit 2

Emoji: From Japan to the World

 日本語から英語に入った言葉をいくつか言えるかな。

 ええっと、sushi, karaoke…。

 tsunami もそうですね。それから…。

 他に kimono、futon などもあるね。でもそんなに多くはない。しかし、絵文字は日本で生まれ世界中に広がったんだよ。

 では絵文字は国際語ということになりますね。

Before Reading
本文を読む前に、以下のタスクに取り組みましょう。

Survey on the Topic
次の1～3について、自分に当てはまるほうを○で囲みましょう。

1. 絵文字は日本で誕生したと知っていた。 [Yes / No]
2. 絵文字は文字より感情をうまく伝えると思う。 [Yes / No]
3. 絵文字を使っていない友達からのメールは冷たい感じがする。 [Yes / No]

Vocabulary
___に適する青色の単語の意味を枠内から選び、記号で答えましょう。

1. communicate effectively ___伝える
2. propose an idea　考えを___
3. inspire people　人々に___
4. weather forecast　天気___
5. universal symbol　___シンボル
6. immediately understand　___理解する
7. complete coincidence　完全な___
8. mobile device　携帯型の___
9. become commonplace　___ものになる
10. beside the message　メッセージ___

| a. ヒントを与える | b. 普遍的な | c. …のそばに | d. 機器 | e. 偶然の一致 |
| f. ありふれた | g. 効果的に | h. 提案する | i. 予報 | j. すぐに |

While Reading 本文をパートごとに読み、あとの問題に答えましょう。

Part 1

 絵文字はいつどのように誕生したのだろうか。英文を読んでみよう。

1 Emoji first **appeared** in Japan in **the late 1990s**, when mobile phones with small, **monochrome displays** became popular. However, only **48 letters** could fit onto the **small screens**. Shigetaka Kurita, who was working for NTT's DoCoMo, **noticed** that people using **pagers** often sent **the symbol of a heart** to **express** their **emotions**. He **realized** that symbols could **communicate meaning** more **effectively** than simple words.

2 Kurita **proposed** the emoji idea to his **bosses**, and then he **developed** 180 emoji. Kurita was **inspired** by the **icons** in **weather forecasts** and the **symbols in manga** to express emotions. Because he realized he was **creating** a new kind of **alphabet**, he tried to make them as **universal** as possible. He hoped that **everyone** would immediately **understand** them when seeing them for the first time. However, Kurita **never imagined** at the time that they would become a **worldwide phenomenon**.

Notes monochrome「単色の」 pager「ポケットベル」 as . . . as possible「できるだけ…」
phenomenon「現象」

Exercises

（1）太字に注意して本文を読み、次の英語の説明と合う単語を探して、提示の語頭に続けて答えましょう。ただし、名詞は単数形を、動詞は原形を書きましょう

1. to start to be seen or known （a　　　　　　　）
2. to create something for some particular purpose （d　　　　　　　）
3. to form a picture or idea in your mind （i　　　　　　　）

（2）本文の内容に合うように空所に適切な単語を記入しましょう。

1. The mobile phones in the late 1990s had small (　　　　　) for only 48 (　　　　　).
2. Shigetaka Kurita found that people expressed their (　　　　　) by sending the symbol of a (　　　　　) on pagers.
3. Shigetaka Kurita thought that (　　　　　) were better at communicating meaning than simple (　　　　　).

（3）空所を補って、本文の内容に関する次の会話を完成させましょう

Saki: 当時の携帯の限られた文字数で、^{1.}＿＿＿＿＿を表すのにシンボルが有効だって気づいた栗田さんはすごいわね。

Kenta: 栗田さんは^{2.}＿＿＿＿＿や、^{3.}＿＿＿＿＿の記号からヒントを得て絵文字を考案したんだね。

Saki: ほんと新しいアルファベットを作るみたい。でも文字と違って絵文字は誰でも^{4.}＿＿＿＿＿ときにわかる！

Kenta: 栗田さんが望んだように絵文字は世界中で^{5.}＿＿＿＿＿的な現象になったんだ。

Thinking Time!

 p.99 の **My Opinion Note A** を使って、自分の立場や意見を答えよう。

Part 2

では、なぜ絵文字が誕生したのが日本なのか、そして実際に世界はどのように絵文字を受け入れているのかについて、さらに英文を読んでみよう。

3 Why is it that emoji were first created and used only in Japan? It may be because *kanji* are like pictures, so Japanese people already have a form of communication through images. Japanese may also have a particular attraction to icons and images, given the popularity of manga and anime.

4 Everyone knows that emoji convey emotions. Therefore, many English speakers may think that the word "emoji" comes from the word "emotion." However, as all Japanese people know, emoji is a word made up of three Chinese characters meaning "picture" plus "character," so the resemblance to the word "emotion" is a complete coincidence.

5 Certainly, emoji have quickly become part of everyone's culture, at least in places where mobile devices are heavily used. In 2015, the Oxford Dictionary named "Face with tears of joy" (😂) its word of the year. As more of the world goes online and mobile, emoji are sure to become more commonplace. The attraction to emoji is clear. The most iconic and popular emoji continues to be the smiling face (☺). No matter what the message says, or in what language it is read, if there is a smiling face emoji beside it, the reader usually feels more relaxed.

Notes given ... 「…を考慮すると」 made up of ... 「…でできている」 Chinese characters 「漢字」
resemblance 「類似」 at least 「少なくとも」 no matter what ... 「何を…しようとも」

Exercises

(4) 本文のキーワードであると思われる語（句）に下線を引きましょう。

(5) 絵文字が日本で誕生した理由について、次の文を完成させましょう。
1. 漢字は＿＿＿＿＿＿なので、日本人はすでに＿＿＿＿＿＿＿＿＿＿＿＿＿を持っているのである。
2. 日本人はまたシンボルやイメージに＿＿＿＿＿＿を感じているのかもしれない。

(6) 下線部は具体的にどのような偶然の一致だと思いますか。次の文を完成させて答えましょう。

漢字の「絵」と「文字」からなる言葉 emoji は英語の＿＿＿＿＿＿＿＿＿＿＿が同じである。

(7) 絵文字が世界で広く受け入れられていることを示す具体例を、次のそれぞれの絵文字について答えましょう。

1. 😂 ＿＿＿＿＿＿＿＿＿＿＿＿＿＿＿＿＿＿＿＿＿＿＿＿＿＿＿＿＿＿＿＿

2. ☺️ ＿＿＿＿＿＿＿＿＿＿＿＿＿＿＿＿＿＿＿＿＿＿＿＿＿＿＿＿＿＿＿＿

Listening Comprehension

Audio 13

ケンタとアビーの絵文字に関する会話を音声で聴き、次の英文が会話の内容に合っていれば T (True)、合っていなければ F (False) を [　] に記入しましょう。

[　] 1. Abbie says that she can communicate with words better than with emoji.

[　] 2. Abbie already knew that emoji is a Japanese word.

[　] 3. Kenta says everyone in the world smiles the same way.

Thinking Time!

p.99 の My Opinion Note B を使って、自分の立場や意見を答えよう。

After Reading

日本語に合うように英文を完成させましょう。なお、下線部に相当する表現は提示しています。

1. できるだけすぐに電話をください。　　　　　　　　　　　　　　　[as . . . as possible]

   Please give me a (　　　　) (　　　　　) (　　　　) (　　　　　)
   (　　　　　).

2. ローマ字は 26 文字でできている。　　　　　　　　　　　　　　　[be made up of . . .]

   The Roman alphabet (　　　　　) (　　　　　) (　　　　　)
   (　　　　) 26 (　　　　　).

3. 少なくとも天気予報では明日は晴れだ。　　　　　　　　　　　　　　　[at least]

   (　　　　) (　　　　　) in the (　　　　　) (　　　　　), it says it
   will (　　　　) (　　　　　) tomorrow.

4. 部屋の大きさを考えれば、もっと大きなエアコンが必要だろう。　　　　[given . . .]

   (　　　　) the (　　　　　) of the (　　　　　), we will
   (　　　　) a (　　　　　) air-conditioner.

5. あなたが何を言おうとも、私はあなたの考えに何の魅力も感じない。[no matter what . . .]

   (　　　　) (　　　　　) (　　　　　) (　　　　　)
   (　　　　　), I feel no (　　　　　) to your ideas.

Unit 3

Tokyo 2020: Chance for a New Beginning

 これまでに何度、日本でオリンピックが開催されたか知っているかい？

1960年代にも東京で開催されたのですよね。

 そして冬季オリンピックも開催されたんだ。

札幌と長野ですね。だから、これまでに3度です。

 その通り。1964年の東京オリンピックは国際オリンピック委員会の会長に史上最高の大会であったと称されたのだよ。

Before Reading　本文を読む前に、以下のタスクに取り組みましょう。

Survey on the Topic　次の1〜3について、自分に当てはまるほうを○で囲みましょう。

1. 東京オリンピックをとても楽しみにしている。　　　　　　　　　　　　[Yes / No]
2. オリンピックにはなるべくお金をかけないほうがよい。　　　　　　　　[Yes / No]
3. オリンピックを機会におもてなしの心を海外に広めたい。　　　　　　　[Yes / No]

Vocabulary　＿＿に適する青色の単語の意味を枠内から選び、記号で答えましょう。

1. remarkably different ＿＿ 異なる
2. devastating defeat 壊滅的な＿＿
3. bring prestige ＿＿をもたらす
4. fierce competition 激しい＿＿
5. cause controversy ＿＿を引き起こす
6. complain about the cost 費用について＿＿
7. recovery efforts ＿＿努力
8. huge deficit 莫大な＿＿
9. occupy the site 場所を＿＿
10. initial design ＿＿設計

| a. 最初の | b. 著しく | c. 競争 | d. 敗北 | e. 論争 |
| f. 赤字 | g. 復興 | h. 占有する | i. 名声 | j. 不平を言う |

While Reading

本文をパートごとに読み、あとの問題に答えましょう。

Part 1

 1964年の東京オリンピックは世界に何を示したのか、そして半世紀以上経って開催される2度目の東京大会は世界に何を示すのだろうか。英文を読んで考えてみよう。

1 The 2020 Tokyo Olympics **arrive** at a time in Japan's history **remarkably different** than the era of the 1964 Games. The first Tokyo Games came when Japan had a lot to **prove**. Less than 20 years earlier, Japan had **suffered** a **devastating defeat** in **World War II**. Although the **economy** then was rapidly **improving**, Japan mostly looked like a **third-world country**. The 1964 Games gave Japanese people the **opportunity** to show the world that they had **rebounded** from their **suffering**.

2 **Unlike** the 1964 Games, the 2020 Games will be held in a **modern**, **hi-tech country** and the **third largest economy** in the world. However, **similar** to the 1964 Games, Japan still has something to **prove**: it has **recovered** from another **devastating event**—the Great East Japan Earthquake.

3 Because the Olympics can **bring** a lot of **prestige** to the **hosting country** and city, the **competition** for **hosting** is usually **fierce**. In 2013, Tokyo **beat** Madrid and Istanbul who had also **reached** the **final round**. In the summer of 2020, Japan, especially Tokyo, will be in the **spotlight**.

Notes　era「時代」　look like ...「…のように見える」　third-world country「第三世界の国」
rebound「立ち直る」　unlike ...「…とは違って」　hosting country「開催国」

Exercises

(1) 太字に注意して本文を読み、次の英語の説明と合う単語を探して、提示の語頭に続けて答えましょう。ただし、名詞は単数形を、動詞は原形を書きましょう。

1. to show something is true by facts　　　　　　　　(p　　　　　　　　)
2. to experience something unhappy　　　　　　　　(s　　　　　　　　)
3. to do better than somebody in a game or a competition　　(b　　　　　　　　)

(2) 次のそれぞれの質問の答えを完成させましょう。

1. What big event did Japan experience before the 1964 Games?
 — They suffered _____ in _____.
2. What was Japan like in 1964?
 — The economy was _____, but Japan looked like _____.
3. What opportunity did Japan have by hosting the 1964 Games?
 — It had the opportunity _____ that _____.

(3) 空所を補って、本文の内容に関する次の会話を完成させましょう。

Kenta: 日本は1964年の大会当時と別の国みたいに変わったんだね。
Saki: ええ、今では 1._____ の国、経済は世界第3位の大国だもの。
Kenta: オリンピックは開催国に 2._____ から、オリンピック開催をかけての 3._____ は激しいんだ。
Saki: 東京に決定したときは日本中が喜んだわ。
Kenta: 次の大会では世界に 4._____ を示さないとね。
Saki: でもお金を使って派手にやるのは反対だわ。
Kenta: そうだね、最終選考で競った 5._____ の人たちにも納得してもらえる大会にしたいね。

Thinking Time!

 p.101 の **My Opinion Note** A を使って、自分の立場や意見を答えよう。

Part 2

 次の東京オリンピックへの準備が進む中、解決していかなければならない問題がいろいろある。それについて、さらに英文を読んでみよう。

4 Holding big events like the Olympics always causes some controversy and the 2020 Games has already produced some challenges. Although most Japanese support the Games this time, some people have complained about their high cost. They claim it would be better to spend money on earthquake recovery efforts. There is also the fear that the Games could result in a huge deficit.

5 Tokyo has a big advantage in holding the Olympics for a second time because many of the same sites for the 1964 Games can be used again. This should save much money, but the 2020 Games will still not be cheap. Although the National Olympic Stadium will occupy the original site, it has to be completely rebuilt. The initial design, which included luxuries such as a retractable roof and air-conditioning, had to be abandoned to save money.

6 Finally, Japan has been facing an economic slump since the 1990s. Thus, the mood of the country is dramatically different now from the early 1960s when there was more optimism about the future. Therefore, the 2020 Games provide an opportunity to show the spirit of the 1964 Games.

Notes challenge「難題」 spend money on...「…にお金を使う」 result in...「…という結果になる」
luxuries「ぜいたくなもの」 such as...「…のような」 retractable「格納式の」
abandon「断念する」 thus「だから」 optimism「楽観論」

Exercises

（4）本文のキーワードであると思われる語（句）に下線を引きましょう。

（5）オリンピックを開催することに反対する人たちの論点について、次の文を完成させて答えましょう。

問題は＿＿＿＿＿＿＿＿＿＿＿＿＿＿＿＿＿＿＿＿＿＿＿＿＿＿＿＿＿で、それよりも

＿＿＿＿＿＿＿＿＿＿＿＿＿＿＿＿＿＿＿＿＿＿＿＿＿＿＿＿＿＿＿＿ほうがよい。

（6）次のそれぞれの書き出しに続けて、筆者が指摘する問題点を完成させましょう。

1. 今回の2度目のオリンピックは1964年大会で使用した場所の多くが使えるので費用を節約できるはずだが、そうもいかない。たとえば…

   国立競技場は＿＿＿＿＿＿＿＿＿＿＿＿＿＿＿＿＿＿＿＿＿＿＿＿＿＿＿＿＿＿。

2. 未来に楽観的であった1960年代前半と比べると…

   1990年代から続く不況のせいで、＿＿＿＿＿＿＿＿＿＿＿＿＿＿＿＿＿＿＿＿＿＿。

Listening Comprehension

ケンタとアビーのオリンピックに関する会話を音声で聴き、次の英文が会話の内容に合っていればT (True)、合っていなければF (False) を [ ] に記入しましょう。

[ ] 1. Kenta is against hosting the Olympic Games.

[ ] 2. Kenta thinks that hospitality is important in hosting the Games.

[ ] 3. Abbie has decided to be in Japan in 2020.

Thinking Time!

p.101 の **My Opinion Note B** を使って、自分の立場や意見を答えよう。

After Reading

日本語に合うように英文を完成させましょう。なお、下線部に相当する表現は提示しています。

1. 新しい競技場は大きなアップルパイ<u>のように見える</u>。　　　　　　　　　　[look like ...]

　　The new (　　　　) (　　　　　　) (　　　　　　) a (　　　　　　)
　　(　　　　　) (　　　　　　).

2. 最初の設計<u>とは違って</u>、この計画は多くのお金を節約できる。　　　　　　[unlike ...]

　　(　　　　　) the (　　　　　) (　　　　　　), this plan (　　　　　　)
　　(　　　　　) a lot of money.

3. 私はぜいたく品<u>にお金を使い</u>たくない。　　　　　　　　　　　　　　　[spend money on ...]

　　I don't (　　　　) (　　　　　) (　　　　　) (　　　　　)
　　(　　　　　) luxuries.

4. 復興の努力は大きな成功<u>という結果になった</u>。　　　　　　　　　　　　　[result in ...]

　　The (　　　　　) (　　　　　) (　　　　　) (　　　　　) a big
　　(　　　　　).

5. 東京<u>のような</u>大都市には多くの異なる種類のレストランがある。　　　　　[such as ...]

　　In big cities, (　　　　　) (　　　　　) (　　　　　　), there are many
　　(　　　　　) (　　　　　) (　　　　　) restaurants.

Unit 4

Pet Obsession

 obsession とはどういう意味ですか。

 何かにとりつかれていることだよ。

 ではペットにとりつかれているってことですか。なんだか恐いですね。

 いやいやそうではなく、この場合はとりつかれるほど夢中になっているということだ。

 ペットに夢中ということですか。

 現在、日本では4世帯に1世帯の割合で何かのペットが飼われているそうだ。

Before Reading
本文を読む前に、以下のタスクに取り組みましょう。

Survey on the Topic
次の1～3について、自分に当てはまるほうを○で囲みましょう。

1. ペットを飼っている。 [Yes / No]
2. 他人のペットのことで迷惑だと感じたことがある。 [Yes / No]
3. ペットを何十万円も払って買うことは理解できない。 [Yes / No]

Vocabulary
____に適する青色の単語の意味を枠内から選び、記号で答えましょう。

1. fictional character ____人物
2. completely realistic まったく____
3. need companionship ____を求める
4. loyalty to owners 飼い主への____
5. exceedingly cute ____かわいい
6. attachment to pets ペットへの____
7. protection of dogs イヌの____
8. get attention ____を得る
9. abandon pets ペットを____
10. animal shelter 動物の____

| a. 保護 | b. 非常に | c. 保護施設 | d. 注目 | e. 捨てる |
| f. 現実的な | g. 仲間づきあい | h. 愛着 | i. 架空の | j. 忠実さ |

While Reading

本文をパートごとに読み、あとの問題に答えましょう。

Part 1

 日本の昨今のペットブームについて英文を読んでみよう。

1 Emiko is a single 42-year-old living in Setegaya-ku, Tokyo with her pet poodle, Koko. Emiko and Koko **wake up together** around 7 a.m. in their futon. Emiko **serves** a breakfast of minced Kobe **beef** to Koko before she eats her own breakfast. She then **dresses** Koko in a new **designer outfit**. She is a bit **disappointed**, however, because Koko is too **fat** to **fit** into the Gucci dog **jacket** she recently **bought**.

2 Although Emiko is a **fictional character**, all of her **activities** are completely **realistic**. Presently Japanese **own** as many as **20 million** cats and dogs, and this number is even **bigger** than the number of Japanese people under 15 years old. The **reasons** for the continuing pet **boom** in Japan are many. Perhaps the **main** reason is the need for **companionship** in a country with increasingly small families. Dogs are especially **well known** for **loyalty** to their **owners**. It also helps that small dogs, such as poodles, are exceedingly **cute**. For many people, their pets have become a **real member** of their family.

> Notes   minced beef「ミンチ牛肉」 designer outfit「ブランドの服」 too ～ to ...「あまりに～で…できない」
> be known for ...「…で知られている」

Exercises

（1）太字に注意して本文を読み、次の英語の説明と合う単語を探して、提示の語頭に続けて答えましょう。ただし、名詞は単数形を、動詞は原形を書きましょう。

1. to stop sleeping （w　　　　　　）
2. to give someone food or drink （s　　　　　　）
3. unhappy because something was unsuccessful （d　　　　　　）

（2）本文の内容に合うように空所に適切な単語を記入しましょう。

1. Koko eats minced Kobe beef for (　　　　　) which Emiko (　　　　　).
2. Emiko is a bit (　　　　　) because she cannot (　　　　　) Koko in the Gucci dog jacket.
3. Emiko is not a real (　　　　　), but what she does is completely (　　　　　).

（3）空所を補って、本文の内容に関する次の会話を完成させましょう

Kenta: ココがうらやましいよ。朝食に神戸牛だよ！
Saki: 大事にされているのはイヌだけじゃないわ。今、日本では ¹._____ よりも多い数のネコやイヌが飼われているのよ。
Kenta: 驚きだね。それにその主な理由が、ますます ²._____ なっていて ³._____ とは。
Saki: イヌは ⁴._____ であることはよく知られているわね。小型犬はかわいいし。多くの飼い主にとって ⁵._____ なのね。飼い主やペットといった言葉は使わないほうがいいかもね。

Thinking Time!

p.103 の My Opinion Note A を使って、自分の立場や意見を答えよう。

Part 2

 しかし、ペットと日本人の関係は今に始まったことではないのだ。さらに英文を読んでみよう。

3　Japan has had a long attachment to pets. Tokugawa Tsunayoshi, for example, was known as the Dog Shogun because of his love and protection of dogs. And of course, almost all Japanese are familiar with the story of Hachiko, the loyal dog whose bronze statue still sits outside Shibuya Station in Tokyo. It is not just dogs and cats that get attention. Japanese are well known for keeping unusual pets, such as beetles and turtles.

4　However, there is a negative side to the pet boom. One of the major problems is the number of abandoned cats and dogs. As they age, dogs, especially, lose their cuteness. In the meantime, many owners discover that their pets need attention, food and health care, and they require time and significant expense. As a result, some owners take their pets to an animal shelter. Sadly, the chance that they will find a new owner is very small. In most cases, they are put down. On the other hand, owners, like Emiko, would never let this happen.

5　Japan's pet obsession is actually not unusual in the world today. In many countries, dogs and cats, more than ever before, are treated like family members. Although most do not get the same treatment as Koko, they still live lives of luxury.

Notes　**Tokugawa Tsunayoshi**「徳川綱吉（徳川幕府第5代将軍）」　**be familiar with ...**「…をよく知っている」
　　　　bronze statue「銅像」　**as a result**「その結果」　**put down**「処分する」

Exercises

（4）本文のキーワードであると思われる語（句）に下線を引きましょう。

（5）日本人が古くからペットに愛着を感じていたことを示す2つの例を、次のそれぞれについてまとめましょう。

1. 将軍徳川綱吉：＿＿＿＿＿＿＿＿＿＿＿＿＿＿＿＿＿＿＿＿＿＿＿＿＿＿＿＿＿＿＿
2. ハチ公：＿＿＿＿＿＿＿＿＿＿＿＿＿＿＿＿＿＿＿＿＿＿＿＿＿＿＿＿＿＿＿＿＿＿

（6）空所を補って、ペットブームのマイナス面についてまとめましょう。

　　ペットが 1.＿＿＿＿＿＿＿＿＿＿。
　→　2.＿＿＿＿＿＿＿＿＿がなくなる。
　→　世話や 3.＿＿＿＿＿＿や 4.＿＿＿＿＿＿面でのケアが必要。
　→　5.＿＿＿＿＿＿＿＿とかなりの 6.＿＿＿＿＿＿＿が必要。
　→　動物保護施設に預ける。
　➡　[結果] ほとんどのペットが 7.＿＿＿＿＿＿＿＿される。

Listening Comprehension

Audio 21

ケンタとアビーのペットブームに関する会話を音声で聴き、次の英文が会話の内容に合っていればT (True)、合っていなければF (False) を [ ] に記入しましょう。

[ ] 1. Abbie says that more than half of American families have pets.

[ ] 2. Abbie says that small dogs are more popular in America than in Japan.

[ ] 3. Kenta feels it is terrible that some owners abandon their pets when they get old.

Thinking Time!

　p.103 の My Opinion Note B を使って、自分の立場や意見を答えよう。

After Reading

日本語に合うように英文を完成させましょう。なお、下線部に相当する表現は提示しています。

1. 新商品の広告はあまりに単純でまったく注目を得られなかった。　　[too ～ to . . .]

   The (　　　　) of the new product (　　　　) (　　　　) simple

   (　　　　) (　　　　) any attention.

2. ハチ公は飼い主への忠実さでよく知られている。　　[be known for . . .]

   Hachiko (　　　　) (　　　　) (　　　　) (　　　　) his

   (　　　　) to his (　　　　).

3. 世界の多くの子どもたちがドラえもんをよく知っている。　　[be familiar with . . .]

   (　　　　) (　　　　) in the world (　　　　) (　　　　)

   (　　　　) Doraemon.

4. 私は何の努力もしなかった。その結果、夢を捨てなければならなかった。　　[as a result]

   I didn't make any (　　　　). (　　　　) (　　　　)

   (　　　　), I had to (　　　　) my (　　　　).

5. そのかわいそうなイヌは飼い主がどこかへ引っ越しするときに処分された。　　[put down]

   The (　　　　) (　　　　) (　　　　) (　　　　)

   (　　　　) when its (　　　　) (　　　　) somewhere.

Unit 5

Silver Japan

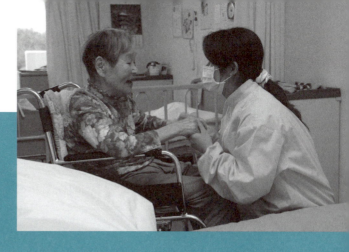

silver Japan、「銀色の日本」ってどういうことですか。

 silver には「白髪」という意味もあり、silver Japan は高齢化した日本のことだよ。国連は 65 歳以上の人口に占める割合が 7% を超えると「高齢化社会」、14% を超えると「高齢社会」、そして 21% を超えると「超高齢社会」と分類している。

アメリカは 14% を少し超えているから「高齢社会」ですね。日本はどうでしょうか。

Before Reading　本文を読む前に、以下のタスクに取り組みましょう。

Survey on the Topic　次の 1 ～ 3 について、自分に当てはまるほうを○で囲みましょう。

1. 「高齢化社会」という言葉にマイナスのイメージを持つ。　　　　　　　　　[Yes / No]
2. 日本は高齢化が進んでいると実感する。　　　　　　　　　　　　　　　　[Yes / No]
3. 高齢化社会に生きる自分はついていないと思う。　　　　　　　　　　　　[Yes / No]

 Vocabulary　＿＿に適する青色の単語の意味を枠内から選び、記号で答えましょう。

1. grim statistics　＿＿統計
2. extreme aging　＿＿高齢化
3. ignore the elderly　高齢者を＿＿
4. affect politics　政治に＿＿
5. replace the position　役職の＿＿
6. job opportunities　職の＿＿
7. health care profession　医療の＿＿
8. expanding careers　＿＿職
9. severe crowding　激しい＿＿
10. financial stress　＿＿ストレス

| a. 影響を与える | b. 経済的な | c. 無視する | d. 混雑 | e. 厳しい |
| f. 拡大する | g. 代わりとなる | h. 極度の | i. 機会 | j. 職業 |

While Reading 本文をパートごとに読み、あとの問題に答えましょう。

Part 1

 現在、日本の人口で65歳以上が占める割合はどれくらいなのだろうか。日本の高齢化の現状について英文を読んでみよう。

1 By now, everyone is well **aware** of Japan's **aging society**. Unfortunately, the **statistics** are rather **grim**. **About 27 percent** of the **population** is now **over 65** years old, and by 2060, **40 percent** will be. This is **a huge change** from 60 years ago. In those days, **almost half** of Japan's population was **under 20**. There are **several reasons** for such an old population: people are having **fewer children** due to the **continuing weak economy**, plus Japan has **few immigrants**; Japanese also have **the longest lifespan** at 83 years.

2 Many countries, such as Italy, Poland, Korea and Taiwan, face a **similar situation**, although not quite as **extreme**. However, the **good news** is that Japan is **treating** its elderly quite well, despite the huge numbers. Unlike the **distant past** when **grandma** was **carried** into the **mountains** and **left to die**, today's elderly are getting **better treatment** than ever. This good treatment is **driven** by **politics** and **economics**. Elderly people in Japan have big **voting** and **purchasing power**; therefore, neither the government nor companies can **ignore** them.

Notes　be aware of ...「…を認識している」　statistics「統計」　due to ...「…のせいで」　lifespan「寿命」
　　　　be driven by ...「…に推進される」　voting「投票」　purchasing「購買」

Exercises

(1) 太字に注意して本文を読み、次の英語の説明と合う単語を探して、提示の語頭に続けて答えましょう。ただし、名詞は単数形を、動詞は原形を書きましょう。

1. all the people who live in an area, city or a country (p　　　　　　)
2. the system of a country's money and goods (e　　　　　　)
3. a way of doing something towards someone (t　　　　　　)

(2) 本文の内容に合うように空所に適切な単語や数字を記入しましょう。

1. By 2060, (　　　　　　) percent of Japanese population will be (　　　　　　) (　　　　　　).
2. In Japan, the number of (　　　　　　) is decreasing because the (　　　　　　) is slowing down.
3. Japan accepts few (　　　　　　) into their society.

(3) 空所を補って、本文の内容に関する次の会話を完成させましょう

Saki:　多くの国で高齢化がみられるけど、日本は「超高齢社会」なのね。
Kenta:　そうだね、日本ではポーランドや韓国と比べて高齢化が １.＿＿＿＿＿＿＿＿ ようだね。
Saki:　高齢化が進むと将来が心配だわ。
Kenta:　でも昔に比べて今の日本では高齢者は ２.＿＿＿＿＿＿＿＿＿＿＿＿。たとえば高齢者は ３.＿＿＿＿＿＿＿＿ に大きな影響を与えるから、４.＿＿＿＿＿＿＿＿ は彼らを無視することはできないんだね。
Saki:　昔はお年寄りを ５.＿＿＿＿＿＿＿＿ って本当の話なのかな。
Kenta:　子どもの頃にそんな物語を読んだことがあるよ。

Thinking Time!

p.105 の My Opinion Note A を使って、自分の立場や意見を答えよう。

Part 2

 高齢化社会にはマイナス面しかないのだろうか。高齢化社会が私たちの暮らしに与える影響について、さらに英文を読んでみよう。

3 Inevitably, however, an aging society does not only affect old people. Because so many workers are retiring, Japan needs young people to replace them. Japan now has one of the lowest unemployment rates in the world. Therefore, young people will have more job opportunities. Also, careers in health care professions are expanding because the elderly need extra care. If you plan to work in a hospital as a doctor, nurse or therapist, you will have no problem finding a career for the rest of your life. There is another advantage: as the number of old people increases, the youth will be able to enjoy trains that are less crowded and roads with fewer traffic jams. Golden Week and *obon* holidays may feel much more enjoyable without severe crowding.

4 On the negative side, however, all of Japan's elderly need to be supported by fewer and fewer young people so taxes need to rise. Today, no young Japanese can remember a time when there was no consumption tax, which began at three percent in 1989. Taxes will have to continue rising to support Japan's aging population. Money for pensions might not even exist in the future.

5 Thus, an aging society has both advantages and disadvantages. Although there will be more employment opportunities for young people, there may also be more financial stress.

Notes　unemployment rate「失業率」　have no problem *do*ing「…するのに困らない」
比較級 and 比較級「ますます…」　consumption tax「消費税」　pension「年金」

Exercises

（4）本文のキーワードであると思われる語（句）に下線を引きましょう。

（5）高齢化社会のプラス面について、次の文を完成させましょう。

　1. 多くの人が定年を迎え、彼らに代わる若者が必要となるので、＿＿＿＿＿＿＿＿＿＿＿＿＿＿＿＿＿。
　2. 高齢者が増えると、＿＿＿＿＿＿＿＿＿＿＿＿＿＿＿＿＿＿＿＿＿＿＿＿＿＿＿＿＿＿＿＿＿。

（6）高齢化社会のマイナス面について、次の文を完成させましょう。

　1. 高齢者を支える若者がますます少なくなるので、＿＿＿＿＿＿＿＿＿＿＿＿＿＿＿＿＿＿＿＿。
　2. 将来、＿＿＿＿＿＿＿＿＿＿＿＿＿＿＿＿＿＿＿＿＿＿＿＿＿＿＿＿＿＿かもしれない。

Listening Comprehension

ケンタとアビーの高齢化社会に関する会話を音声で聴き、次の英文が会話の内容に合っていればT (True)、合っていなければF (False)を [　] に記入しましょう。

[　] 1. Kenta thinks that there are no advantages in an aging society.
[　] 2. Kenta says that his parents didn't have to pay any consumption tax when they were young.
[　] 3. Abbie says that society has been the same since their parents were young.

Thinking Time!

p.105 の **My Opinion Note** B を使って、自分の立場や意見を答えよう。

After Reading

日本語に合うように英文を完成させましょう。なお、下線部に相当する表現は提示しています。

1. 私たちは日本の経済が直面している厳しい状況のことを認識している。　[be aware of ...]

   We ( ) ( ) ( ) the ( ) situation of Japan's ( ).

2. 激しい雪のせいで、ものすごい交通渋滞があった。　[due to ...]

   ( ) ( ) the heavy ( ), there was an extreme ( ) ( ).

3. 将来の仕事を決めるときは、給料だけに動かされるべきではない。　[be driven by ...]

   When you decide on your ( ) ( ), you should not ( ) ( ) only ( ) the salary.

4. この辺りでは、アパートを見つけるのに困らないでしょう。　[have no problem *doing*]

   You will ( ) ( ) ( ) ( ) an apartment around this area.

5. 近頃ますます多くの外国人が日本を訪れる。　[比較級 and 比較級]

   These days, ( ) ( ) ( ) ( ) from other countries ( ) ( ).

Unit 6

Changing Gender Roles

 アビー、女性解放運動が起こった国アメリカでは、今やほとんどの職種に女性が進出しているね。

はい、言葉についても男女の差別をなくそうといろいろ変化がありました。

 たとえば policeman が police officer、fireman が firefighter のような例があるね。

それなら日本語でもありますよ。看護婦という言葉はもう使われなくて、看護師です。

 日本でもそれまでの固定化された男女の役割に変化が起きているようだね。

Before Reading 本文を読む前に、以下のタスクに取り組みましょう。

Survey on the Topic 次の1～3について、自分に当てはまるほうを○で囲みましょう。

1. 女性のタクシードライバーに違和感を持つ。　　　　　　　　　　[Yes / No]
2. 女性の警官は男性の警官より頼りにならない。　　　　　　　　　[Yes / No]
3. 看護師や保育士は女性のほうが適している。　　　　　　　　　　[Yes / No]

 ### Vocabulary ___ に適する青色の単語の意味を枠内から選び、記号で答えましょう。

1. **towards** a seat   座席____
2. female **lawyer**   女性の____
3. **slice** fish   魚を____
4. role **reversal**   役割の____
5. **pour** a drink   飲み物を____
6. **delicate** women   ____女性
7. **handle** the stress   ストレスに____
8. men's **behavior**   男性の____
9. take **priority**   ____を持つ
10. fall into a **trap**   ____に落ちる

| a. 弁護士 | b. 優先権 | c. …の方へ | d. 薄切りにする | e. 対処する |
| f. 繊細な | g. わな | h. 行動、態度 | i. 注ぐ | j. 逆転 |

— 43 —

While Reading

本文をパートごとに読み、あとの問題に答えましょう。

Part 1

 日本の昨今の男女の役割の変化について英文を読んでみよう。

1 You **enter** a sushi restaurant. A loud **welcome** immediately **greets** your ears, but something sounds **strange**. You move towards a seat at the counter and sit down. Then you **notice** something really **unusual**. The sushi **master** is a young **woman**. Welcome to the world of **shifting gender roles**.

2 Among all **professions** in Japan, the sushi **chef** is almost always **male**. You will sometimes see **female taxi drivers** and **lawyers**, but to see a woman **slicing fish** and **molding rice** behind the counter at a sushi restaurant is still **rare**. However, increasingly in Japan, women are **serving** in **roles** that were once **exclusive** to men.

3 Now **consider** another **role reversal**. **Imagine** your father doing the following **chores** at **home**: When you get up in the morning, you see him in the **kitchen** with his apron on **preparing** *miso* soup. In the evening, you **arrive** home and **smell** rice cooking, and again your father is there, still in his apron **preparing dinner**. Later in the evening, your father **pours** a **drink** for your mother and then **reads** a bedtime **story** to your sister. Perhaps this **description** sounds **unbelievable**, but the **fact** is, Japanese men are taking more **responsibility** in **family life**.

Notes mold「形作る」 exclusive to ...「…に限定の」 chore「雑用」 description「描写」
the fact is ...「実際は…である」 take responsibility「責任を持つ」

Exercises

（1）太字に注意して本文を読み、次の英語の説明と合う単語を探して、提示の語頭に続けて答えましょう。ただし、名詞は単数形を、動詞は原形を書きましょう。

1. to say hello to someone or welcome them　　　　　　（ g　　　　　　　）
2. to change from one position or state to another　　　（ s　　　　　　　）
3. not seen or found very often　　　　　　　　　　　　（ r　　　　　　　）

（2）著者が述べる日本の現状について、次のそれぞれの質問に英語で答えましょう。

1. Do you see female taxi drivers more than female sushi chefs?
   — _____

2. Are there more women who take men's role than before?
   — _____

3. Are Japanese fathers the same as ever?
   — _____

（3）空所を補って、本文の内容に関する次の会話を完成させましょう。

Saki:　私は女性がおすしを握っていてもまったく違和感ないけど。

Kenta:　すし職人は伝統的に男性だからね。最近は女性の ^{1.}_____ や ^{2.}_____ は増えてきたけど。かつては ^{3.}_____ だった職種にも女性が進出してきているのは確かだね。

Saki:　家庭でも役割の ^{4.}_____ が起きているっていうことは、今までの日本の父親は家事をしなかったのね。父親が家族の生活に ^{5.}_____ ようになってきたという当たり前のことが話題になるのが問題だと思うわ。

Thinking Time!

p.107 の **My Opinion Note** A を使って、自分の立場や意見を答えよう。

Part 2

 いわゆる「育メン」が好意的に受け入れられる現代は数十年前までの日本とは大きく変わりつつある。なぜこのような変化が起きているのか。さらに英文を読んでみよう。

4 Changing gender roles may be accelerating in Japan. There are many old beliefs increasingly viewed as nonsense: women's hands are too warm to mold sushi rice, women are too delicate to handle the stress of being a pilot and women are not strong enough to be members of the Self-Defense Forces. All of these are now considered (A)<u>old thinking</u>.

5 The reasons for a change in men's behavior are plain to see. Most new parents in their 20s and 30s remember growing up and watching their own fathers leave early for work and return after they had gone to bed. Most new fathers, and of course their wives, realize that their fathers' lifestyle was out of balance because work was taking priority over their family. Thus, they want to avoid falling into (B)<u>the same trap</u>.

6 Although the change in gender roles is happening very slowly, it certainly makes sense. Just as women can be great sushi chefs, men can also be great parents and housekeepers. In the near future, it may be more common to see male nurses and female train drivers in Japan.

Notes　accelerate「加速する」　Self-Defense Forces「自衛隊」　avoid *doing*「…することを避ける」
　　　　make sense「道理にかなっている、意味をなす」

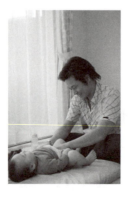

Exercises

（4）本文のキーワードであると思われる語（句）に下線を引きましょう。

（5）下線部 (A) の具体例を、次のそれぞれの書き出しに続けて完成させましょう。

1. 女性の手は＿＿＿＿＿＿＿＿＿＿＿＿＿＿＿＿＿＿＿＿＿＿＿＿＿＿＿。
2. 女性は繊細過ぎて＿＿＿＿＿＿＿＿＿＿＿＿＿＿＿＿＿＿＿＿＿＿＿。
3. 女性は十分に強くないので＿＿＿＿＿＿＿＿＿＿＿＿＿＿＿＿＿＿＿。

（6）下線部 (B) を、次のキーワードをすべて日本語にして用いて説明しましょう。

[out of balance   work   priority   family]

＿＿＿＿＿＿＿＿＿＿＿＿＿＿＿＿＿＿＿＿＿＿＿＿＿＿＿＿＿＿＿＿＿＿
＿＿＿＿＿＿＿＿＿＿＿＿＿＿＿＿＿＿＿＿＿＿＿＿＿＿＿＿＿＿＿＿＿＿
＿＿＿＿＿＿＿＿＿＿＿＿＿＿＿＿＿＿＿＿＿＿＿＿＿＿＿＿＿＿＿＿＿＿

Listening Comprehension

ケンタとアビーの男女の役割に関する会話を音声で聴き、次の英文が会話の内容に合っていれば T (True)、合っていなければ F (False) を [　] に記入しましょう。

[　] 1. Kenta says it looks strange to see a female sushi chef.
[　] 2. Kenta says he will do chores at home when he gets married.
[　] 3. Kenta believes in his father's way of life as his model.

Thinking Time!

 p.107 の My Opinion Note B を使って、自分の立場や意見を答えよう。

After Reading

日本語に合うように英文を完成させましょう。なお、下線部に相当する表現は提示しています。

1. 緑色の席は高齢者<u>限定</u>だ。　　　　　　　　　　　　　　　　　　　　　[exclusive to . . .]

　　The green seats (　　　　) (　　　　　) (　　　　　) (　　　　　)

　　(　　　　　).

2. <u>実は</u>、私はアルコールをまったく飲まない。　　　　　　　　　　　　　　[the fact is]

　　(　　　　) (　　　　　) (　　　　　), I (　　　　　)

　　(　　　　) alcohol (　　　　　) (　　　　　).

3. 彼が新しいプロジェクトに対して<u>全責任を持っている</u>。　　　　　　　[take responsibility]

　　He is (　　　　　) all (　　　　　) for the (　　　　　)

　　(　　　　　).

4. 私は 12 時を過ぎて寝ることを<u>避ける</u>ようにしている。　　　　　　　　　[avoid *do*ing]

　　I try to (　　　　　) (　　　　　) (　　　　　) bed after 12:00.

5. 父のアドバイスはいつも<u>道理にかなっている</u>。　　　　　　　　　　　　　[make sense]

　　My father's (　　　　　) (　　　　　) (　　　　　) (　　　　　).

Unit 7

Maternity Harassment

 マタニティーハラスメントってマタハラのことですよね。ハラスメントってどういうことですか。

 ハラスメントは「嫌がらせ」のことだ。マタニティー、つまり妊婦への嫌がらせのことだよ。

 英語では maternity harassment とは言わず、pregnancy discrimination という言葉が使われます。妊娠によって受ける差別のことです。

 職場でのマタハラを男女雇用機会均等法違反として最高裁が判断した事例もあるのだよ。

Before Reading　本文を読む前に、以下のタスクに取り組みましょう。

Survey on the Topic　次の1〜3について、自分に当てはまるほうを○で囲みましょう。

1. マタハラという言葉の意味を知っていた。　[Yes / No]
2. 妊婦の仕事を同僚が助けるのは当然だと思う。　[Yes / No]
3. マタハラを受けた場合、訴訟を起こすべきだ。　[Yes / No]

 Vocabulary　＿＿に適する青色の単語の意味を枠内から選び、記号で答えましょう。

1. time of celebration ＿＿の時
2. colleague at work 職場の＿＿
3. special treatment 特別な＿＿
4. lack understanding 理解を＿＿
5. cruel remark ＿＿発言
6. threaten the job 仕事を＿＿
7. fire an employee 従業員を＿＿
8. allow leave 休暇を＿＿
9. legal process ＿＿経過
10. receive criticism ＿＿を受ける

a. 残酷な	b. 祝賀	c. 許可する	d. 解雇する	e. 同僚
f. 法的な	g. 脅かす	h. 欠く	i. 扱い	j. 批判

— 49 —

While Reading 本文をパートごとに読み、あとの問題に答えましょう。

Part 1

 日本のマタハラの現状について英文を読んでみよう。

1　When a **baby** is **born** anywhere in the world, it is **normally** a time of **celebration**. In Japan, however, when a future mother **announces** that she is **pregnant** to her **colleagues** at work, there is sometimes **no celebration**. In fact, the **opposite** may **occur**. This **phenomenon** has come to be known as *matahara*, or **maternity harassment**.

2　In the Japanese **workplace**, maternity harassment can come in **many forms**, both **mild** and **severe**. **Refusing** to give the pregnant employee any **special treatment** at all could be called a mild form. For example, early in a pregnancy, mothers-to-be often get **morning sickness**, and they may be **late for work**. Some employees **lack understanding** for this **lateness**.

3　A more **serious**, but similar harassment occurs when other employees make **cruel remarks**, such as, "We have to **work harder** because of you," or "I wish I could arrive at work at 10 a.m.," or even "You are so **selfish**." These kinds of comments can be considered a form of **bullying**.

Notes　normally「通常は」　pregnant「妊娠している」　in fact「実際には」　come to *do*「…するようになる」
　　　　　at all「(肯定文や疑問文で) ともかくも、少しでも」　mother-to-be「未来の母」
　　　　　morning sickness「つわり」　because of ...「…のために」　bullying「いじめ」

Exercises

(1) 太字に注意して本文を読み、次の英語の説明と合う単語を探して、提示の語頭に続けて答えましょう。ただし、名詞は単数形を、動詞は原形を書きましょう。

1. to officially tell people something　　　　　　　　(a　　　　　　　)
2. to happen, take place　　　　　　　　　　　　　(o　　　　　　　)
3. to say that you will not do something　　　　　　(r　　　　　　　)

(2) 本文の内容に合うように空所に適切な単語を記入しましょう。

1. When a woman says she is pregnant in the workplace, there is sometimes no (　　　　　) from her (　　　　　).
2. There are many (　　　　　) of *matahara*, both (　　　　　) and (　　　　　).
3. Pregnant women sometimes receive no (　　　　　) (　　　　　) at work.

(3) 空所を補って、本文の内容に関する次の会話を完成させましょう

Saki:　　子どもが生まれるのは祝福されるべきことなのにマタハラだなんて。
Kenta:　体調が優れないせいで遅刻しても、同僚の中には ^{1.}＿＿＿＿＿＿＿＿＿＿人もいるんだね。
Saki:　　それどころではないわ。「君のせいで ^{2.}＿＿＿＿＿＿＿＿＿＿＿」とか「自分も ^{3.}＿＿＿＿＿＿＿＿＿＿＿」や「君は ^{4.}＿＿＿＿＿＿＿＿＿＿＿」などのひどい発言をする人もいるのね。
Kenta:　それはもう ^{5.}＿＿＿＿＿＿＿＿と言っていいね。

Thinking Time!

p.109 の **My Opinion Note A** を使って、自分の立場や意見を答えよう。

Part 2

 さらに英文を読んで、個人の問題としてだけでなく、日本社会の問題としてマタハラを考えてみよう。

4 The most severe type of harassment occurs when a pregnant employee feels her job is threatened. The boss may demote the new mother or refuse to allow any maternity leave. In the worst case, the new mother may even be fired. Of course, firing or even refusing maternity leave is illegal in Japan. There are labor laws protecting working women who become pregnant and give birth, but these are not fully enforced in Japan.

5 One recent famous case, however, may be showing that the situation in Japan is improving. In Hiroshima, a therapist in a hospital was demoted after announcing to her boss that she was pregnant. Therefore, she sued the hospital. After a long legal process, the case went to the Supreme Court and the woman won. Amazingly, after winning, the woman did not want her name publicized or her photo taken because she received so much criticism from the public. This reveals that there is still much to improve in Japanese attitudes towards working women.

6 In the end, in the 21st century, for the country's economy, Japanese should change their usual way of treating women in the workplace. Women should have the freedom to continue working while pregnant and afterwards. They should not fear they will lose their post or status in their workplace.

Notes　enforce「施行する」　demote「降格させる」　maternity leave「産休」
in the worst case「最悪の場合には」　labor law「労働法」　give birth「出産する」
sue「訴える」　Supreme Court「最高裁判所」　publicize「公表する」
reveal「明らかにする」　there is still much to *do*「まだ…すべきことが多くある」
continue *do*ing「…し続ける」

Exercises

(4) 本文のキーワードであると思われる語（句）に下線を引きましょう。

(5) 下線部の例を、以下のそれぞれのキーワードをヒントにして日本語で答えましょう。

1. demote: _____
2. maternity leave: _____
3. fire: _____

(6) 空所を補って、広島での事例をまとめましょう。

病院に勤める 1._____ が妊娠を 2._____ に告げる。
→ 病院は女性を 3._____ させる。
→ 女性は病院を 4._____ て、5._____ まで行った裁判で女性が 6._____ 。
→ 女性は 7._____ ことを拒否。世間から 8._____ ことが理由。

Listening Comprehension

ケンタとアビーのマタハラに関する会話を音声で聴き、次の英文が会話の内容に合っていれば T (True)、合っていなければ F (False) を [　] に記入しましょう。

[　] 1. Abbie says *matahara* is rare in America.
[　] 2. Kenta says pregnant women should not be demoted.
[　] 3. Abbie says not only the couple but society also needs children.

Thinking Time!

 p.109 の My Opinion Note B を使って、自分の立場や意見を答えよう。

After Reading

日本語に合うように英文を完成させましょう。なお、下線部に相当する表現は提示しています。

1. 私は彼をよい人だと思っていたが、実際はデリカシーに欠けている。　　　　　　　　　[in fact]

    I (　　　　　) he was a (　　　　　) (　　　　　　), but (　　　　　　)

    (　　　　　), he (　　　　　) delicacy.

2. インターネットは世界中で利用されるようになった。　　　　　　　　　　　　　　[come to *do*]

    The Internet has (　　　　　) (　　　　　) (　　　　　) (　　　　　　)

    all over (　　　　　) (　　　　　).

3. 大衆からの厳しい批判のために、その政治家は引退を決意した。　　　　　　　　[because of . . .]

    The politician has (　　　　　) to retire (　　　　　) (　　　　　　) severe

    (　　　　　) from the (　　　　　).

4. 最悪の場合、私は徹夜で勉強しなければならないかもしれない。　　　　　　　[in the worst case]

    (　　　　) (　　　　) (　　　　) (　　　　　), I might

    (　　　　) (　　　　) (　　　　　) all night.

5. 夕食後もテレビを見続けたので、私は宿題を終えることができなかった。

    　　　　　　　　　　　　　　　　　　　　　　　　　　　　　　　　　　　[continue *doing*]

    I couldn't (　　　　　) my (　　　　　) because I (　　　　　)

    (　　　　) (　　　　　) (　　　　　) (　　　　　).

Unit 8

Digital Youth: The Connected Generation

 電話を切ることを英語では hang up と言うね。

 でも hang up って「つるす」ってことですよね。

 電話が発明された当初、切るときは受話器を壁に掛けた電話機につるしたことから hang up が「切る」という意味になったのだよ。

 今や携帯電話が主流で、タッチして切る時代です。

 ずっと携帯を触っている人たちなら、文字通り hang up することはなくなった。

 connected generation、接続されている世代ですね。

Before Reading　本文を読む前に、以下のタスクに取り組みましょう。

Survey on the Topic　次の1〜3について、自分に当てはまるほうを○で囲みましょう。

1. 携帯を家に忘れると不安になる。　　　　　　　　　　　　　　　　[Yes / No]
2. 1時間に1度は携帯をチェックする。　　　　　　　　　　　　　　[Yes / No]
3. 携帯がなくなったら自分の生活は大きく変わると思う。　　　　　　[Yes / No]

 ### Vocabulary　＿＿に適する青色の単語の意味を枠内から選び、記号で答えましょう。

1. seek an identity　独自性を＿＿
2. creative way　＿＿やり方
3. addicted to phone　電話に＿＿
4. incoming message　＿＿メッセージ
5. post a message　メッセージを＿＿
6. be depressed　＿＿いる
7. physical health　＿＿健康
8. health concern　健康の＿＿
9. stare at a screen　画面を＿＿
10. enough exercise　十分な＿＿

| a. 落ち込んで | b. 創造的な | c. 運動 | d. 凝視する | e. 体の |
| f. 探求する | g. 投稿する | h. 入ってくる | i. 中毒になった | j. 心配 |

While Reading 本文をパートごとに読み、あとの問題に答えましょう。

Part 1

 携帯世代の現状について英文を読んでみよう。

1 Young people today / are never unconnected. / Mobile technology has given us phones / that have almost become part of our bodies. / Today's youth are the first generation / to grow up / in an always-connected world. / This is a huge difference / from their parent's generation. /

2 One unique characteristic / of today's social networks / is their real-time, / ever-present nature. / Whether it is during class, / lunch time / or when doing homework, / many young people are aware / when a new message comes in. / Some even sleep / with their mobile phone / beside their pillow / so they can check their networks / and respond / in the middle of the night. /

3 There are several reasons / for this super connectivity. / Teenagers are building / a personal identity. / Social networks with friends / are ideal platforms / for seeking an identity. / Another reason / is related to the new culture of participation. / Groups of friends / play games / or share information / such as music, photos and videos. / They often mix the information together / in a creative way, / such as using stickers. / Thus, / people can share with their group members / using the new technology. / A third reason is related to the need / to belong to a group, / which is very important / in Japanese culture. /

Notes ever-present「途切れることのない」 whether ...「…であっても（なくても）」
so (that) + S + (can) V「SがVできるように」 in the middle of ...「…のただ中で、途中で」
personal identity「独自性」 platform「拠点となる場所」 thus「このようにして」
share with ...「…に参加する、…と共有する」

Exercises

(1) / の区切りごとに意味をとって本文を読み、次の英語の説明と合う単語を探して、提示の語頭に続けて答えましょう。ただし、名詞は単数形を、動詞は原形を書きましょう。

1. all people of about the same age　　　　　　　　　　(g　　　　　　　)
2. to give a spoken or written answer　　　　　　　　　(r　　　　　　　)
3. the act of taking part in an activity　　　　　　　　　(p　　　　　　　)

(2) 本文の内容に合うように空所に適切な単語を記入しましょう。

1. Young people today are much different from their parent's (　　　　　　) because they are always (　　　　　　).
2. It is (　　　　　　) (　　　　　　) that has made young people different from their parents.
3. Mobile phones have almost become part of our (　　　　　　), so we can (　　　　　　) whenever a message comes in.

(3) 空所を補って、本文の内容に関する次の会話を完成させましょう

Kenta: 携帯でほとんどいつも誰かと <u>1.　　　　　　　　　　</u>、そんな社会で僕たちは育ったんだね。親の世代との大きな違いだ。

Saki: 常に携帯をそばに置いてチェックし、真夜中でも <u>2.　　　　　　　　　　</u>。

Kenta: 友人とのソーシャルネットワークは <u>3.　　　　　　　　　　</u>する理想的な場になっているとはどういうことだろう。

Saki: 他者とのコミュニケーションを通して自己を見つめるということかな。

Kenta: 友人たちと音楽や写真、動画などの <u>4.　　　　　　　　　　</u>するのも楽しいしね。

Saki: そうね、そして <u>5.　　　　　　　　　　</u>ということも日本の文化では大事なこと、そう言われればそうね。でも試しに1日、携帯なしで生活してみようかな。

Thinking Time!

 p.111 の My Opinion Note A を使って、自分の立場や意見を答えよう。

Part 2

 常に携帯がそばにあって、いつも誰かと連絡が取れることは便利だが、その弊害もあるようだ。さらに英文を読んでみよう。

4 Naturally, being connected all the time also has its disadvantages. Some youths become addicted to their phones and networks. Hearing the sound or feeling the vibration of an incoming message becomes almost like a drug and they sometimes ignore their studies. Also, because most people post only good things about themselves, it is easy to become depressed about seeing everyone always having a good time.

5 There are also physical health concerns associated with constantly using mobile phones. Staring down at a small screen for hours can be hard on the eyes and the neck. Moreover, if you are always sitting down using your phone, you are unlikely to get enough exercise.

6 Finally, although today's parents complain about young people using their phones too much, they may have forgotten about their own behavior when they were young. At that time, their own parents may have complained about them watching too much TV and talking too long on the phone. Therefore, in one sense, today's connected youth are actually not so different from their parents. However, in those days, when they hung up the phone, the connection was cut.

Notes　vibration「振動」　be unlikely to *do*「…しそうにない」　may have + 過去分詞「…したかもしれない」
in one sense「ある意味で」

Exercises

(4) 本文を、意味の区切りごとに / を入れて読みましょう。

(5) 下線部の具体的な内容を、以下のそれぞれのキーワードをヒントにして日本語で答えましょう。

1. addicted: _____
   _____

2. depressed: _____
   _____

3. physical health concern: _____
   _____

(6) 空所を補って、本文で述べられている「現代の若者と親の世代の比較」を完成させましょう。

親の世代：1._____ と 2._____ のため、3._____ から文句を言われた。
現代の若者：4._____ のため、5._____ から文句を言われる。

それゆえ ↓

両世代は 6._____ いない。

しかし ↓

親の世代は電話を切れば、7._____ も切られた。

Listening Comprehension
Audio 37

ケンタとアビーの携帯世代に関する会話を音声で聴き、次の英文が会話の内容に合っていれば T (True)、合っていなければ F (False) を [ ] に記入しましょう。

[   ] 1. Kenta always carries his phone with him.
[   ] 2. Kenta thinks there is nothing bad about using his phone.
[   ] 3. Abbie says using phones is good for studies and exercise.

Thinking Time!

 p.111 の My Opinion Note B を使って、自分の立場や意見を答えよう。

After Reading

日本語に合うように英文を完成させましょう。なお、下線部に相当する表現は提示しています。

1. 明日が日曜でも休日でも、私は家で歴史の課題を仕上げなければならない。 [whether . . .]

   (   ) (   ) (   ) (   ) or a
   (   ), I have to (   ) my (   ) assignment
   (   ) (   ).

2. 授業の途中で受信したメッセージをチェックすべきではない。 [in the middle of . . .]

   We (   ) (   ) (   ) (   ) messages
   (   ) (   ) (   ) (   ) class.

3. 彼はいつも快活で、こんな些細なことで落ち込みそうにない。 [be unlikely to do]

   He is always (   ), so he (   ) (   )
   (   ) become (   ) about (   ) (   )
   small thing.

4. 彼女から返事がない。私のメッセージを無視したのかもしれない。 [may have + 過去分詞]

   I received no (   ) (   ) her. She (   )
   (   ) (   ) my message.

5. 私はいつもマンガを持ち歩いている。ある意味、マンガに中毒なのだ。 [in one sense]

   I (   ) (   ) manga. (   ) (   )
   (   ), I am (   ) (   ) it.

Unit 9

Japan's Peaceful Poor

日本は貧困層が少ない国ですよね、ジパング博士。

 さあ、それはどうだろうね。

富豪は少ないかもしれませんが、ほとんどの人が食べ物や住む場所に困っていないと思います。

 確かに国民全体が中流といわれた時代もあったが。

そうじゃないのですか。それに「平和な貧困」ってどういうことですか。

Before Reading
本文を読む前に、以下のタスクに取り組みましょう。

Survey on the Topic
次の1～3について、自分に当てはまるほうを○で囲みましょう。

1. 日本は先進国の中で貧困層は少ないほうだと思う。　　　　[Yes / No]
2. 貧困は個人の責任だと思う。　　　　[Yes / No]
3. スリやひったくりの被害にあったことがある。　　　　[Yes / No]

Vocabulary
＿＿に適する青色の単語の意味を枠内から選び、記号で答えましょう。

1. cut off the electricity ＿＿を止める
2. pay the bill ＿＿を払う
3. construction worker ＿＿労働者
4. irregular worker ＿＿労働者
5. wealth and poverty ＿＿と貧困
6. luxury products ＿＿品
7. dine in Ginza 銀座で＿＿
8. prevent crime 犯罪を＿＿
9. culture of patience ＿＿の文化
10. expiry date ＿＿の日

a. 食事をする	b. 富	c. がまん	d. 防止する	e. 電気
f. 建設	g. 期限切れ	h. 非正規の	i. 請求額	j. ぜいたく

― 61 ―

While Reading 本文をパートごとに読み、あとの問題に答えましょう。

Part 1

 日本の貧困の現状について英文を読んでみよう。

1 Chiemi, / a 42-year-old single mother, / lives with her 12-year-old daughter / in a one-room apartment. / She earns 1,000 yen an hour / working as a waitress / in a restaurant, / but she works only six hours / a day. / Her electricity / has been cut off / for the past two weeks / because she missed several payments. / When she gets her monthly salary / in a few days, / she will pay the bill / and her lights will come on again. / In the meantime, / her daughter does her homework / under a candle light. /

2 Hiroshi is a 31-year-old construction worker / who lives in Kotobuki-cho, / Yokohama. / He is single / and lives in a cheap hostel. / Since Hiroshi lost his full-time job / when his company restructured, / he makes a living / by getting casual jobs / on construction sites. / As an irregular worker, / he often works / only three to four days a week. / This means / his salary, / like Chiemi's, / does not reach the poverty line. /

3 In Japan, / that line is set / at half the national median salary. / Presently, / the poverty line / is a bit above 1 million yen / a year, / which means / 16 percent of Japanese are officially poor, / and this percentage / is increasing each year. /

Notes　a day「1日につき」　in the meantime「そうしている間」　hostel「簡易宿泊所」
make a living「生計を立てる」　poverty line「貧困線」
national median salary「国民の所得の中央値」

Exercises

(1) / の区切りごとに意味をとって本文を読み、次の英語の説明と合う単語を探して、提示の語頭に続けて答えましょう。ただし、名詞は単数形を、動詞は原形を書きましょう。

1. to receive money for the work you do (e　　　　　　)
2. to fail to do something (m　　　　　　)
3. to organize something in a new and different way (r　　　　　　)

(2) 次のそれぞれの質問の答えを完成させましょう。

1. Why does Chiemi's daughter have to do her homework under a candle light?
   —The electricity ＿＿＿＿＿＿＿＿＿＿ because Chiemi ＿＿＿＿＿＿＿＿＿＿.
2. Why did Hiroshi lose his full-time job?
   —Because ＿＿＿＿＿＿＿＿＿＿＿＿＿＿＿＿＿＿＿＿.
3. How does Hiroshi make a living?
   —He works on ＿＿＿＿＿＿＿＿ as an ＿＿＿＿＿＿＿＿ three or four days ＿＿＿＿＿＿＿＿.

(3) 空所を補って、本文の内容に関する次の会話を完成させましょう。

Saki: チエミさんもヒロシさんも、働いているのに生活に困っているのね。
Kenta: チエミさんは 1.＿＿＿＿＿＿＿＿＿＿＿まで電気が使えない。
Saki: ヒロシさんは 2.＿＿＿＿＿＿＿＿＿＿＿で暮らしていて 3.＿＿＿＿＿＿＿にも到達しない収入だって。
Kenta: その言葉を初めて聞いたよ。日本では 4.＿＿＿＿＿＿＿＿＿＿＿に設定されていて、額は 5.＿＿＿＿＿＿＿＿＿＿＿くらいなんだね。
Saki: 日本人の 6.＿＿＿＿＿＿＿が貧困で、しかもその割合が増え続けているなんて驚きだわ。

Thinking Time!

 p.113 の **My Opinion Note** A を使って、自分の立場や意見を答えよう。

Part 2

 さらに英文を読んで、他の多くの国とは異なる「平和な貧困」の意味を考えてみよう。

4 Similar to many other countries, Japan has its extremes of wealth and poverty. While wealthy people shop for luxury products and dine in places such as Ginza or Harajuku, the poor just try to survive in places like Kotobuki-cho. The number of poor people is actually huge, so Japan can no longer call itself a "middle-class country." Casual and part-time workers now make up almost 40 percent of all Japanese workers.

5 In some ways, Japan is unlike many other countries with high poverty rates. Poverty sometimes leads to crime. However, even in places like Kotobuki-cho, the crime rate remains low. This may be because the police and government have been successful in preventing crime. It may also be related to Japan's culture of patience (*gaman*).

6 Because of this large population of poor people, several bestselling self-help books provide tips on how to survive on little money. A few of the more unusual tips include: reusing the water after rinsing rice; eating *okara* instead of *tofu*; and buying discounted food on its expiry date. Although these tips may appear extreme, at least poverty is helping Japan produce less waste.

7 In a sense, Japan is not unlike many other countries in the 21st century. A common expression in English is: "the rich get richer and the poor get poorer." This seems to be a trend in today's world.

Notes　**no longer ...**「もはや…ではない」　**middle-class**「中流の」　**poverty rate**「貧困率」
　　　　　lead to ...「…に至る、つながる」　**remain ...**「…のままである」　**be related to ...**「…と関係している」
　　　　　tip「コツ」　**less**「より少ない（little の比較級）」

Exercises

(4) 本文を、意味の区切りごとに / を入れて読みましょう。

(5) 下線部のように筆者が述べている理由を、次のキーワードをすべて日本語にして用いて説明しましょう。

[extremes   wealth   poverty   casual and part-time workers   40 percent]

_____

_____

_____

(6) 空所を補って、筆者が日本の貧困が「平和な貧困」であるとする理由を完成させましょう。

1. 時に貧困は ^{A.}_____ につながるが、日本は ^{B.}_____ が低い。

    理由：①日本の ^{C.}_____ と ^{D.}_____ が ^{E.}_____ に成功している。

    　　　②日本の ^{F.}_____ に関係がある。

2. いかにして ^{G.}_____ のコツを書いた本が売れる。

    そのコツの例：① ^{H.}_____ の再利用。

    　　　　　　　② ^{I.}_____ ではなく ^{J.}_____ を食べる。

    　　　　　　　③ ^{K.}_____ 食品を買う。

Listening Comprehension

ケンタとアビーの貧困に関する会話を音声で聴き、次の英文が会話の内容に合っていればT (True)、合っていなければF (False) を [ ] に記入しましょう。

[   ] 1. The poverty rate of America is higher than that of Japan.

[   ] 2. Abbie says that poverty is related to crime.

[   ] 3. Abbie says patience could cause crime.

Thinking Time!

p.113 の My Opinion Note B を使って、自分の立場や意見を答えよう。

After Reading

日本語に合うように英文を完成させましょう。なお、下線部に相当する表現は提示しています。

1. 私たちの家族は<u>1日に</u>2袋のゴミを出す。　　　　　　　　　　　　　　　[a day]

   (　　　　) (　　　　　　) produces (　　　　　) (　　　　　　) of waste (　　　　) (　　　　　).

2. 授業まで2時間ある。私は<u>その間に</u>課題を終えよう。　　　　　　[in the meantime]

   There are (　　　　　) (　　　　　) (　　　　　) the class. I (　　　　) (　　　　　) the assignment (　　　　　) (　　　　　) (　　　　　).

3. 私は何度か支払いを怠ったので<u>もう電気は使えない</u>。　　　　　　　　[no longer . . .]

   I (　　　　) (　　　　　) (　　　　　　), so I can (　　　　　) (　　　　　) use (　　　　　).

4. その野球選手は努力が成功に<u>つながる</u>と信じて一生懸命に練習してきた。　[lead to . . .]

   The (　　　　) (　　　　　) has been (　　　　　) (　　　　　　), believing effort will (　　　　　) (　　　　　) (　　　　　).

5. あなたは、富は幸福と<u>関係している</u>と思いますか。　　　　　　　　[be related to . . .]

   Do you think that (　　　　　) (　　　　　) (　　　　　) (　　　　　) (　　　　　)?

Unit 10

The Idol-Making Machine

 サキ、君にとってのアイドルは誰かね。

 アイドルですか。私はあまりテレビを見ないですから…。

 どうしてテレビを見ないからアイドルがいないの？
カリフォルニアにいる私のおばあさんは私のアイドルよ。

 おばあさんがアイドル！ おばあさんがアイドルになれるの？

 サキには不思議だろうね。日本語の「アイドル」は英語の本来の意味と違うのだよ。

Before Reading
本文を読む前に、以下のタスクに取り組みましょう。

Survey on the Topic
次の1～3について、自分に当てはまるほうを○で囲みましょう。

1. 応援しているアイドルがいる。 [Yes / No]
2. アイドルは歌や演技が下手でも大きな問題ではない。 [Yes / No]
3. アイドルになりたいと思ったことがある。 [Yes / No]

Vocabulary
___ に適する青色の単語の意味を枠内から選び、記号で答えましょう。

1. specific meaning ___ 意味
2. entertainment industry 娯楽 ___
3. trivial thing ___ こと
4. image of innocence ___ のイメージ
5. meaningless lyrics ___ 歌詞
6. have potential ___ を持つ
7. sign a contract ___ にサインする
8. destroy an image イメージを ___
9. profit much 多く ___
10. envy the idol アイドルを ___

a. 清純	b. 無意味な	c. うらやむ	d. 特定の	e. 産業
f. 潜在能力	g. ささいな	h. 儲ける	i. 壊す	j. 契約（書）

While Reading 本文をパートごとに読み、あとの問題に答えましょう。

Part 1

 英語の本来の意味とは異なる日本のアイドルについて英文を読んでみよう。

1. In English, / an "idol" is a person / who is greatly loved, / so my grandmother / could easily be my idol. / In Japan, / however, / the word "idol" / has a much more specific meaning. /

2. An idol in Japan / could never be a grandmother; / rather, / almost all Japanese idols are young, / and they also must be cute, / or at least cool. / And it goes without saying / that all idols are in the entertainment industry, / which means / they are usually famous. /

3. Although idols are in the entertainment field, / quite often as singers, / they may not be particularly talented. / Young boys and girls are recruited / because of their good looks, / rather than their great voices. / Generally, / the songs they sing / or their roles in movies and TV series / are quite trivial. / Among idols, / having an image of innocence / is also essential. / This is where the story about idols / becomes interesting. /

Notes　it goes without saying that . . .「…は言うまでもない」　entertainment field「芸能界」

Exercises

(1) / の区切りごとに意味をとって本文を読み、次の英語の説明と合う単語を探して、提示の語頭に続けて答えましょう。ただし、名詞は単数形を、動詞は原形を書きましょう。

1. having a natural ability to do something well　　　　(t　　　　　)
2. to find new people to work in a company or an organization　(r　　　　　)
3. very important and necessary　　　　　　　　　　　　(e　　　　　)

(2) 本文の内容に合うように空所に適切な単語を記入しましょう。

1. Unlike the original meaning of "(　　　　　　)," in Japan, the word has a more (　　　　　　) meaning.
2. In Japan, idols are usually (　　　　　　) performers in the (　　　　　　) (　　　　　　).
3. In Japan, idols are recruited because of their (　　　　　　) (　　　　　　), but they may not be particularly (　　　　　　).

(3) 空所を補って、本文の内容に関する次の会話を完成させましょう

Saki:　英語ではアイドルとは **1.**_____人のことで、アビーのおばあさんがアビーのアイドルでもまったく不思議ではないってことね。

Kenta:　そういうことだね。でも日本では **2.**_____にいる、若くてかわいい人やかっこいい人で、彼らの **3.**_____や **4.**_____は大抵さいなものだ。

Saki:　そう言われればそのとおりね。そして大事なことは **5.**_____を持っていること。

Kenta:　日本語のアイドルは英語の本来の意味と違うんだ。

Thinking Time!

p.115 の My Opinion Note A を使って、自分の立場や意見を答えよう。

Part 2

 日本のアイドルの現実について、さらに英文を読んでみよう。

4 Unlike talented artists who become famous because of their musical or acting ability, idols are carefully manufactured by idol-making machines. Talent agencies are specialists at finding very cute pre-teenage boys and girls and training them for several years before introducing them to the public. The songs they sing are specially written for them. Their melodies are upbeat and their lyrics are often either flippant or meaningless.

5 Because idols have the potential to make so much money for their talent agencies, nothing can be left to chance. The agencies have their future idols sign contracts when they are young, and then the agencies tightly control their lives. They are often not allowed to have boyfriends or girlfriends because if their fans found out, it would destroy the image of their idol. Many fans, it seems, have fantasies about dating their idol.

6 Life for an idol may not be as enjoyable as many believe. They spend long hours learning to dance and sing songs. With such hard work, one would imagine that idols enjoy high salaries. The reality, however, is that their talent agencies are profiting the most. This is because idols are locked into contracts signed when they were much younger. Therefore, in most cases <u>there is no need to envy the idol</u>. Their lives are usually much tougher than that of the average person.

7 On the other hand, the fame they enjoy for a brief few years during their youth is something very few people will ever experience. In that sense, being an idol is not all bad.

Notes acting ability「演技力」 talent agency「芸能事務所」 pre-teenage「思春期前の（9〜12歳の）」
either A or B「AかBのどちらか」 flippant「軽々しい」
have＋O＋動詞の原形「Oに…させる［してもらう］」 fantasy「幻想」 lock「閉じ込める」
there is no need to *do*「…する必要はまったくない」 tough「きつい」 fame「名声」
not all ...「すべてが…というわけではない」

Exercises

(4) 本文を、意味の区切りごとに / を入れて読みましょう。

(5) 空所を補って、idol-making machine がアイドルを生産する過程を完成させましょう。

芸能事務所が ^{1.}＿＿＿＿＿＿＿＿＿＿＿＿＿＿を見つける。
→ 数年間、彼らを ^{2.}＿＿＿＿＿＿＿＿＿。
→ 世間に ^{3.}＿＿＿＿＿＿＿＿＿する。

(6) 下線部のように筆者が述べている理由を、次のキーワードをすべて日本語にして用いて説明しましょう。

[contract   control   lives   long hours   learning   talent agency   profit]

_____
_____
_____
_____

Listening Comprehension

ケンタとアビーのアイドルに関する会話を音声で聴き、次の英文が会話の内容に合っていればT (True)、合っていなければF (False) を [　] に記入しましょう。

[　] 1. Kenta feels strange that Abbie's idol is her grandmother.
[　] 2. Abbie understands how idols are manufactured in Japan.
[　] 3. It is talent agencies that Kenta envies.

Thinking Time!

p.115 の My Opinion Note B を使って、自分の立場や意見を答えよう。

After Reading

日本語に合うように英文を完成させましょう。なお、下線部に相当する表現は提示しています。

1. 水は生命にとって<u>不可欠であることは言うまでもない</u>。　　[it goes without saying that ...]

   (　　　　　) (　　　　　　) (　　　　　　) (　　　　　　　)
   (　　　　　) (　　　　　　) is (　　　　　　) for life.

2. 日本への観光客の<u>すべてが英語を話せるというわけではない</u>。　　[not all ...]

   (　　　　　) (　　　　　　) (　　　　　　) to Japan (　　　　　)
   (　　　　　) (　　　　　　).

3. 将来、私は東京か<u>大阪のどちらか</u>の食品産業で働きたい。　　[either A or B]

   In the (　　　　　), I'd like to (　　　　　) for the (　　　　　)
   (　　　　　) (　　　　　) in Tokyo (　　　　　) in Osaka.

4. 専門家に<u>その機械を修理してもらったら</u>どうですか。　　[have＋O＋動詞の原形]

   Why (　　　　　) (　　　　　) (　　　　　) a specialist (　　　　　)
   the (　　　　　)?

5. この洗濯機は使えるよ。新しいのを<u>買う必要はまったくない</u>。　　[there is no need to *do*]

   We (　　　　　) (　　　　　) this washing (　　　　　). (　　　　　)
   (　　　　　) (　　　　　) (　　　　　) (　　　　　)
   (　　　　　) a (　　　　　) one.

- 72 -

Unit 11

Japanese Hospitality: Second to None

 hospitality って「おもてなし」のことですね、ジパング博士。

そうだね、オリンピックの誘致のスピーチで有名になった言葉だね。

日本のお店に行くと女王様になった気分になることがあります。

女王様！そんなふうに思ったことは一度もないわ。でも second to none ってどういうことですか。

 none の次ってことだから…？

あ、「誰にも負けない」ってことですね！

Before Reading
本文を読む前に、以下のタスクに取り組みましょう。

Survey on the Topic
次の 1 ～ 3 について、自分に当てはまるほうを○で囲みましょう。

1. 店員の言葉遣いで腹が立ったことがある。　　　　　　　　　　　　[Yes / No]
2. 「おもてなしの心」は日本の誇りだ。　　　　　　　　　　　　　　[Yes / No]
3. 自分は「おもてなしの心」を持っている。　　　　　　　　　　　　[Yes / No]

Vocabulary
＿＿に適する青色の単語の意味を枠内から選び、記号で答えましょう。

1. polite language ＿＿言葉
2. treat graciously ＿＿扱う
3. illustrate the point　要点を＿＿
4. find a product ＿＿を見つける
5. place a focus ＿＿を置く
6. examine the manual　手引書を＿＿
7. interaction with customers　客との＿＿
8. concept of hospitality　もてなしの＿＿
9. service provider　サービス＿＿
10. enough reward 十分な＿＿

| a. ていねいな | b. 概念 | c. 提供者 | d. 調べる | e. 製品 |
| f. 報酬 | g. 説明する | h. 焦点、重点 | i. 優雅に | j. やりとり |

While Reading

本文をパートごとに読み、あとの問題に答えましょう。

Part 1

 日本の客への対応について読んでみよう。

1　When entering certain types of businesses / as a customer / in Japan, / it is quite common / to be treated very well. / Salespeople usually use / especially polite language / and treat you graciously, / often with a loud welcome. / In some cases, / you may be served tea or coffee / immediately after you are seated. / Welcome to the Japanese world of *omotenashi*, / or hospitality. /

2　Growing up in Japan, / people tend to be unaware / of the special nature / of Japanese hospitality. / However, / once they leave the country / for the first time / and experience service / as a customer outside of Japan, / they may realize / that Japanese hospitality is special indeed. /

3　The following example / illustrates this point. / Enter a large shop / in most countries outside of Japan / and ask a clerk / where to find a certain product. / The clerk is likely to simply tell you / where the product is. / In Japan, / however, / in a similar situation, / the clerk will likely personally take you / to it. / Small, but significant differences like this / reveal Japan's focus on hospitality. / While in English / there is an expression, / "the customer is king," / in Japanese, / the expression is, / "the customer is God." /

Notes　business「（可算名詞で用いて）店、企業」　once ...「一度…すれば」　where to *do*「どこで…するか」

Exercises

(1) / の区切りごとに意味をとって本文を読み、次の英語の説明と合う単語を探して、提示の語頭に続けて答えましょう。ただし、名詞は単数形を、動詞は原形を書きましょう。

1. in private, not officially (p   )
2. to make something known to others (r   )
3. things that people say, write or do in order to show their feelings, opinions and ideas
 (e   )

(2) 本文の内容に合うように次の質問に英語で答えましょう。

1. When you enter a Japanese store, will you usually be spoken to in polite language?
 — _____

2. When you are in Japan, is it easy to know what is special about Japanese hospitality?
 — _____

3. When you are outside of Japan, will you be able to better realize what Japanese hospitality is like?
 — _____

(3) 空所を補って、本文の内容に関する次の会話を完成させましょう

Kenta: アビーが週末にデパートに買い物に行ったんだって。日本で商品の置いてある場所をたずねたら、店員が 1._____って聞いていたらしく、実際にそうだったって感激していたよ。

Saki: アメリカでは違うの？

Kenta: アメリカではたいてい 2._____だけだよ。こんな小さな違いでも日本がおもてなしに 3._____いることがわかるよね。

Saki: 私には当たり前のように思えることだけど。

Kenta: 英語では「お客は 4._____」っていう言葉があるらしいけど、日本では「お客様は 5._____」って言うからね！

Thinking Time!

p.117 の My Opinion Note A を使って、自分の立場や意見を答えよう。

Part 2

 日本の「おもてなし」はどこが特別なのか、さらに英文を読んでみよう。

4　In what ways is Japanese hospitality special? To answer this question, let's examine the training manual received by the employees of retail companies. Inside, every interaction with customers is usually covered: greeting, thanking, apologizing and even the degree of bowing.

5　Japanese hospitality is now expanding abroad because of companies such as Uniqlo and Muji. Both of these companies started in Japan and now have a large part of their businesses overseas. Because the concept of hospitality is so refined in Japan, these companies send their Japanese staff overseas to countries such as Australia to train the local people. In this way, Japanese hospitality is being spread abroad.

6　However, Japanese-style hospitality goes beyond simply treating customers well. Hospitality in Japan is actually like a way of thinking. Treating guests well is part of the culture. The service provider expects nothing in return for the best hospitality given to customers. This may be why tipping is rare in Japan. In North America, tips of about 15 percent are expected by waiters, hairdressers and taxi drivers among others, in return for normal service; however, in Japan, service providers are trained to believe that a happy customer is a good enough reward in itself.

Notes　retail company「小売業の会社」　refined「洗練されている」　go beyond ...「…を超えている」
　　　　　in return for ...「…の見返りに」　this is why ...「これが…である理由だ」

Exercises

(4) 本文を、意味の区切りごとに / を入れて読みましょう。

(5) 空所を補って、海外へ広がる日本のおもてなしについてまとめましょう。

小売業における ¹_____ の接客訓練：あいさつ、²_____、³_____、
⁴_____ の角度など。

↓

成功した小売業（例：⁵_____ や ⁶_____）が ⁷_____ へ進出。

↓

⁸_____ が現地で従業員を訓練。

(6) 空所を補って、客からの見返りに関する北米と日本の違いをまとめましょう。

サービスを ¹_____ 者は、北米では普通のサービスで
²_____ を客から期待するが、日本では見返りに ³_____、
⁴_____ が ⁵_____ だと訓練を受ける。

Listening Comprehension

Audio 49

ケンタとアビーの日本のサービスに関する会話を音声で聴き、次の英文が会話の内容に合っていれば T (True)、合っていなければ F (False) を [ ] に記入しましょう。

[ ] 1. Abbie says Japanese hospitality is the best in the world.

[ ] 2. Kenta says Japanese hospitality is very special.

[ ] 3. Abbie says Japanese service providers should ask for some tips in return for their services.

Thinking Time!

p.117 の **My Opinion Note** B を使って、自分の立場や意見を答えよう。

After Reading

日本語に合うように英文を完成させましょう。なお、下線部に相当する表現は提示しています。

1. いったん教室に入ったら、授業が終わるまで出ることはできません。　　　　[once ...]

   (　　　　) (　　　　　) (　　　　　　) the classroom, you cannot

   (　　　　) (　　　　　) (　　　　　　) it (　　　　　　) the class is

   over.

2. どこでタクシーに乗れるか教えていただけますか。　　　　[where to *do*]

   (　　　　) (　　　　　) (　　　　　) me (　　　　　　)

   (　　　　　) take a (　　　　　)?

3. 私は、その新製品は消費者の期待以上だろうと思う。　　　　[go beyond ...]

   I believe that the (　　　　　) (　　　　　) will (　　　　　)

   (　　　　　) consumers' (　　　　　).

4. 手伝ってもらったお返しに、何でも欲しいものを買ってあげるよ。　　　　[in return for ...]

   (　　　　) (　　　　　) (　　　　　) the (　　　　　), I will

   (　　　　　) you anything (　　　　　) (　　　　　).

5. これが日本のマンガが海外に広まった理由だ。　　　　[this is why ...]

   (　　　　) (　　　　　) (　　　　　　) Japanese manga has

   (　　　　　) (　　　　　).

Unit 12

Shrinking Cities: Returning the Countryside to Nature

 ジパング博士、shrink は「縮む」という意味ですよね。町が縮むってどういうことですか。

 文字通りの意味だよ。町がだんだんと小さくなっていくことだ。

 面積でなくて人口のことですね。

 その通り。日本の人口の半分以上が東京、大阪、名古屋を入れた三大都市圏に住んでいる。それ以外の地域ではどんどん人口が減っているところが多いのだよ。

 そして住む人がいなくなり自然に帰ってしまうってことですか。

Before Reading
本文を読む前に、以下のタスクに取り組みましょう。

Survey on the Topic
次の1〜3について、自分に当てはまるほうを○で囲みましょう。

1. 自分の故郷は人口が減っている。　　　　　　　　　　　　　　[Yes / No]
2. 暮らすには都会はいなかより魅力的だと思う。　　　　　　　　[Yes / No]
3. 国の政策は地方の町より人口の多い都市に重点を置くべきだ。　[Yes / No]

Vocabulary
＿＿に適する青色の単語の意味を枠内から選び、記号で答えましょう。

1. a dozen people　　＿＿人々
2. struggle to survive　生き残るために＿＿
3. Japanese diet　日本人の＿＿
4. decreasing population　＿＿人口
5. demand for rice　米の＿＿
6. attract people　人を＿＿
7. make an effort　＿＿をする
8. maintain a community　コミュニティを＿＿
9. rural area　＿＿地域
10. establish a reputation　＿＿を確立する

| a. 需要 | b. 引きつける | c. 12(人)の | d. 評判 | e. 努力 |
| f. 維持する | g. 減少する | h. 食生活 | i. いなかの | j. 苦闘する |

While Reading 本文をパートごとに読み、あとの問題に答えましょう。

Part 1

 北海道の夕張市を例に過疎化する町について読んでみよう。

1　Most people in Japan / have heard of Yubari, / a town in Hokkaido / famous for its delicious melons. / However, / Yubari is becoming famous / for something else: / it has the oldest population / in Japan. / It may even have the oldest population / in the world. / In 2020, / the median age will be about 65 years / with more people over 80 / than under 40. / For every baby born in Yubari, / a dozen people die. / Sadly, / in Yubari, / this means more diapers are sold / for the elderly / than for babies. /

2　Contrast Yubari with Tokyo. / While Tokyo feels full of activity and energy / every day and night, / Yubari has few people / walking along its streets, / and at night / it feels like a ghost town. / The shops and companies / struggle to survive. / If you start a business in Yubari, / you should sell canes or silver walkers / rather than snowboards and sports cars. / As for employment opportunities, / it is much better / to be a nurse / than an elementary school teacher. /

Notes　the median age「年齢の中央値」　diaper「おむつ」　cane「杖」　silver walker「シルバーカー」
as for ...「…については」

Unit 12　Shrinking Cities: Returning the Countryside to Nature

Exercises

(1) / の区切りごとに意味をとって本文を読み、次の英語の説明と合う単語を探して、提示の語頭に続けて答えましょう。ただし、名詞は単数形を、動詞は原形を書きましょう。

1. to compare two things, ideas, people, etc.　　　　　(c　　　　　　)
2. to continue to live or exist　　　　　　　　　　　　(s　　　　　　)
3. concerning the first stages of a course of study　　　(e　　　　　　)

(2) 本文の内容に合うように空所に適切な単語を記入しましょう。

1. It is Yubari that has the oldest population in (　　　　　　), and possibly in the (　　　　　　) as well.
2. In Yubari, the number of people over (　　　　　　) will be larger than those under (　　　　　　) in 2020.
3. The number of deaths will be (　　　　　　) times as great as that of newborn (　　　　　　).

(3) 空所を補って、本文の内容に関する次の会話を完成させましょう。

Saki:　　メロンで有名な夕張市が人口の高齢化の問題を抱えているのね。
Kenta:　2020年には ¹·＿＿＿＿＿＿＿＿がちょうど真ん中の年齢になる予想だね。
Saki:　　東京は毎日昼も夜も ²·＿＿＿＿＿＿＿＿＿＿＿＿＿＿＿＿＿なのに、夕張は夜は
　　　　　³·＿＿＿＿＿＿＿＿＿みたいだって。
Kenta:　夕張で商売を始めるなら、スノーボードやスポーツカーを売るより、
　　　　　⁴·＿＿＿＿＿＿＿＿＿＿＿＿＿＿を売ったほうがいいって。
Saki:　　仕事を探すなら、⁵·＿＿＿＿＿＿＿＿＿＿＿より看護師ね。

Thinking Time!

 p.119 の My Opinion Note A を使って、自分の立場や意見を答えよう。

Part 2

 町の過疎化の原因とその対策について、さらに英文を読んでみよう。

3 Many shrinking villages and small towns depend on rice farming. However, as the Japanese diet is changing and the population is decreasing, there is less demand for rice. Also, young people are attracted by jobs in big cities and they don't want to get their hands dirty. Japan's fishing villages are experiencing a similar decline for the same reason. Young Japanese would rather work behind a desk than get up at four o'clock in the morning and head out to stormy seas.

4 The government has made efforts to help small communities maintain post offices, fire stations and police departments. In some communities, innovative ideas, such as growing food organically, have brought new life to rural areas. Such fruit and vegetables can be sold as luxury products both domestically and abroad, where Japanese foods have established a reputation for high quality.

5 However, despite <u>such efforts</u>, many of Japan's towns and villages will probably disappear and nature will slowly take over. On the outskirts of Yubari where tens of thousands of coal workers once lived, the valley is now completely green. Some parts of Japan will gradually begin to look a bit like the land seen by the first people arriving on the archipelago thousands of years ago.

Notes　depend on . . .「…に依存する」　rice farming「稲作農業」　decline「衰退」
would rather *do*「むしろ…したい」　head out to . . .「…に向かって進む」
innovative「革新的な」　organically「有機栽培で」　domestically「国内で」
take over「支配する、引き継ぐ」　outskirt「郊外」
tens of thousands of . . .「何万の…、極めて多くの…」
coal worker「炭鉱労働者」　archipelago「島国」

Exercises

(4) 本文を、意味の区切りごとに / を入れて読みましょう。

(5) 空所を補って、過疎化に至る原因を完成させましょう。

1. 村や町が A._____ に依存。
   → B._____ の変化と C._____ の減少。
   → D._____ の低下。
   → 産業の停滞。

2. 若者が E._____ に魅力を感じる。
   → 労働力の低下。

(6) 空所を補って、本文の下線部の例を完成させましょう。

1. 政府が過疎化地域の A._____ の存続を助ける。

2. 一部の地域では B._____ 農作物を高級品として C._____ で売り、D._____ としての評判を確立する。

Listening Comprehension

ケンタとアビーの過疎化に関する会話を音声で聴き、次の英文が会話の内容に合っていればT (True)、合っていなければF (False) を [　] に記入しましょう。

[　] 1. Kenta wants to work outside of Tokyo.

[　] 2. Abbie says Japanese should make sushi with ingredients from abroad.

[　] 3. Kenta will think about becoming a farmer or a fisherman.

Thinking Time!

p.119 の My Opinion Note B を使って、自分の立場や意見を答えよう。

After Reading

日本語に合うように英文を完成させましょう。なお、下線部に相当する表現は提示しています。

1. 品質に関しては、日本製品は世界で評判が良い。　　　　　　　　　　　[as for . . .]

   (　　　　　) (　　　　　　) (　　　　　　　), Japanese (　　　　　　　) have a

   good (　　　　　　) (　　　　　　) (　　　　　　　) (　　　　　　).

2. 外国からの労働者に依存している日本企業もある。　　　　　　　　　[depend on . . .]

   Some Japanese (　　　　　　) (　　　　　　) (　　　　　　) (　　　　　　)

   from (　　　　　　) countries.

3. 私はどこかの会社に勤めるよりむしろ商売を始めたい。　　　　　　　[would rather do]

   I (　　　　　　) (　　　　　　) (　　　　　) a (　　　　　　) than work

   for a (　　　　　　).

4. 私は父から稲作を引き継ぐつもりだ。　　　　　　　　　　　　　　　[take over . . .]

   I'm going to (　　　　　　) (　　　　　　) (　　　　　　) (　　　　　　)

   from (　　　　　　) (　　　　　　).

5. 何万もの人々が東京ドームでポール・マッカートニーのライブを楽しんだ。
   　　　　　　　　　　　　　　　　　　　　　　　　　　[tens of thousands of . . .]

   (　　　　　　) (　　　　　) (　　　　　　) (　　　　　　)

   (　　　　　　) (　　　　　　) Paul McCartney's live performance at Tokyo Dome.

Unit 13

Student Power: The New Youth Movement

2016年に法改正がなされて18歳から選挙権を持つようになったね。

はい、私はもう有権者です。では、この student power って政治に与える力のことですね。

その通り。選挙は国民が直接政治に影響を与える重要な手段だ。

僕たちもよい日本の未来を築くためにいろいろ考えないといけないですね。

そのためには、まず日本や世界の現状をよく知ることが大事だね。

Before Reading　本文を読む前に、以下のタスクに取り組みましょう。

Survey on the Topic　次の 1 〜 3 について、自分に当てはまるほうを○で囲みましょう。

1. すでに投票したことがある。　　　　　　　　　　　　　　　[Yes / No]
2. 政治のニュースをよく読む。　　　　　　　　　　　　　　　[Yes / No]
3. 日本の未来に不安を感じている。　　　　　　　　　　　　　[Yes / No]

Vocabulary　＿＿に適する青色の単語の意味を枠内から選び、記号で答えましょう。

1. **march** on campus　キャンパスを＿＿
2. **violent** clash　＿＿衝突
3. be sent to **prison**　＿＿へ送られる
4. government's **proposal**　政府の＿＿
5. right to **vote**　＿＿権利
6. **election** result　＿＿結果
7. **generate** change　変化を＿＿
8. **previous** year　＿＿年
9. **political** viewpoint　＿＿見解
10. Japanese **politician**　日本の＿＿

| a. 刑務所 | b. 選挙 | c. 生み出す | d. 提案 | e. 暴力的な |
| f. 政治の | g. 投票する | h. 政治家 | i. 前の | j. 行進する |

While Reading 本文をパートごとに読み、あとの問題に答えましょう。

Part 1

 日本の学生による運動の過去と現在について英文を読んでみよう。

1 Half a century ago, / the Japanese university scene / was far different from today. / Huge groups of students / marched on campuses / around the country. / Classes were often boycotted, / and university buildings / were sometimes occupied by students. / Violent clashes with police / took place / on many campuses / and thousands of students / were arrested, / and some were even sent / to prison. / In the late 1960s, / on university campuses / in many countries / students were very politically active / usually taking anti-government / and anti-war positions. /

2 Since that time, / students in Japan / have been relatively quiet and non-political. / However, / this silence / may be coming to an end. / Recently, / students have been forming groups / and speaking out about causes / that they believe in. / One group, / called "SEALDs," / disliked the Japanese government's proposal / to change the interpretation of the constitution / in order to let the Self-Defense Forces fight abroad. / There is one main difference / from the 1960s, / however; / SEALDs took a non-violent approach / to its protests. /

Notes   relatively「比較的」 come to an end「終わりになる」 cause「主義、主張」
believe in ...「…を(よいと)信じる」 interpretation of the constitution「憲法の解釈」
approach「方法、取り組み方」

Exercises

(1) / の区切りごとに意味をとって本文を読み、次の英語の説明と合う単語を探して、提示の語頭に続けて答えましょう。ただし、名詞は単数形を、動詞は原形を書きましょう。

1. for the police to take someone to a police station because they think the person may have committed a crime (a   )
2. a complete lack of noise or sound (s   )
3. something you do to show that you think something is wrong (p   )

(2) 本文の内容に合うように空所に適切な単語を記入しましょう。

1. About 50 years ago, some university students (   ) classes and (   ) university buildings.
2. In the late 1960s, a number of students were (   ) by police and some of them were sent to (   ).
3. Many students in the late 1960s were against their (   ) and (   ), that is, they were politically active.

(3) 空所を補って、本文の内容に関する次の会話を完成させましょう

Kenta: アメリカでも 1.＿＿＿＿＿＿代にベトナム戦争に反対して学生運動が起こったけど、当時は日本でも同じだったんだね。

Saki: その後、日本の学生はずっと 2.＿＿＿＿＿＿＿＿＿＿＿＿＿＿。でも最近は違ってきているわ。

Kenta: グループを作って、3.＿＿＿＿＿＿＿＿＿＿＿について声に出すようになったんだ。街でデモをしている大勢の学生を見たよ。

Saki: 4.＿＿＿＿＿＿＿＿＿＿＿＿＿＿＿という政府の提案に反対するデモね。

Kenta: また逮捕される学生が出たのかな？

Saki: 1960年代と違うところは、5.＿＿＿＿＿＿＿＿＿＿＿＿をとっていることよ。

Thinking Time!

 p.121 の My Opinion Note A を使って、自分の立場や意見を答えよう。

Part 2

 日本の若者が政治に与える影響について、さらに英文を読んでみよう。

3 This new activism among students comes at a time when the voting age has been lowered to 18 years. When the voting age was 20 years, Japan was actually quite unusual as most countries in the world had already set the age at 18. This lowering of the age could result in a significant change because Japanese have traditionally viewed adulthood as beginning at 20. However, Japanese society may be recognizing that childhood is ending earlier. Thus, young people could influence election results if they vote. But is this influence realistic?

4 At present, the reality is that Japan is a silver democracy. Eighteen and 19 year-olds represent only about two percent of the population. It is questionable whether such a small percentage can really generate significant change. This is especially because many new adults have spent the previous year studying for exams rather than forming political viewpoints. Thus, they may not even bother to vote.

5 In order to bring about change, it may be more realistic for today's youth to form groups such as SEALDs. They get plenty of media coverage and the attention of politicians. The youth movement of the 1960s and 1970s shows that students can achieve real positive change. It is up to the present youthful generation to lead the way.

Notes activism「行動主義」 lower「下げる」 adulthood「成人期」 bother to *do*「わざわざ…する」
bring about ...「…をもたらす」 media coverage「マスコミの報道」 up to ...「…次第で」

Exercises

(4) 本文を、意味の区切りごとに / を入れて読みましょう。

(5) 空所を補って、筆者が述べている選挙権の年齢引き下げについての<u>肯定的</u>な見解を完成させましょう。

- 世界の多くの国の ¹.＿＿＿＿＿＿＿＿＿＿＿＿＿＿＿＿は 18 歳。
- 日本社会が子ども時代は ².＿＿＿＿＿＿＿＿＿＿＿＿＿＿＿と認識。
- → 日本における選挙権取得年齢の ³.＿＿＿＿＿＿＿＿。
- → 若者が投票すれば、⁴.＿＿＿＿＿＿＿＿＿＿＿＿＿＿だろう。

(6) 空所を補って、筆者が述べている選挙権の年齢引き下げについての<u>否定的</u>な見解を完成させましょう。

- 日本は ¹.＿＿＿＿＿＿＿が多い民主主義国家。
- 18、19 歳の若者が ².＿＿＿＿＿＿＿＿＿＿＿＿は約 2 パーセント。
- 18、19 歳の若者の多くは、前年には ³.＿＿＿＿＿＿＿＿＿＿＿＿よりも、試験のための勉強をしていた。
- → ⁴.＿＿＿＿＿＿＿＿＿＿＿＿＿＿＿＿＿は疑問だ。

Listening Comprehension

（Audio 57）

ケンタとアビーの若者の政治への関心に関する会話を音声で聴き、次の英文が会話の内容に合っていれば T (True)、合っていなければ F (False) を [ ] に記入しましょう。

[   ] 1. Kenta didn't vote because he didn't have the right.

[   ] 2. Abbie says American youth talk about politics a lot.

[   ] 3. Kenta is going to learn about politics more.

Thinking Time!

p.121 の My Opinion Note B を使って、自分の立場や意見を答えよう。

After Reading

日本語に合うように英文を完成させましょう。なお、下線部に相当する表現は提示しています。

1. 大学の寮で一人暮らしを始めたときに私の子ども時代は終わった。　　　[come to an end]

   My childhood (　　　) (　　　) (　　　) (　　　)

   when I (　　　) (　　　) (　　　) alone in a college dorm.

2. あなたは民主主義の力を信じていないのですか。　　　[believe in . . .]

   Don't you (　　　) (　　　) the (　　　) of (　　　)?

3. こんなに暑い日曜日にわざわざ街を行進したのですか。　　　[bother to do]

   Did you (　　　) (　　　) (　　　) (　　　) the

   street on (　　　) (　　　) hot Sunday?

4. あなたの努力がよい結果をもたらすといいですね。　　　[bring about . . .]

   I hope that (　　　) (　　　) will (　　　) (　　　)

   a (　　　) (　　　).

5. 次の金曜日にディナーパーティーをするかどうかはあなた次第です。　　　[up to . . .]

   It is (　　　) (　　　) (　　　) whether we will

   (　　　) a dinner party (　　　) (　　　).

Unit 14

Japan in Space: Leaping to New Frontiers

フロンティアとは未開拓の土地や分野のことですね、ジパング博士。

そうだね。人類は地球のフロンティアがなくなると宇宙へと飛び出した。

1960年代、アメリカはロシア、当時のソ連と競争してロケットを打ち上げていました。

最初に人間を宇宙に送り込んだのがソ連、そして人間を月面に着陸させたのがアメリカですね。

その通り。でも日本も研究や技術面では当初からずっと貢献してきたんだ。

Before Reading 本文を読む前に、以下のタスクに取り組みましょう。

Survey on the Topic 次の1〜3について、自分に当てはまるほうを○で囲みましょう。

1. 宇宙の話に興味を持っている。 [Yes / No]
2. いつか宇宙から地球を見てみたい。 [Yes / No]
3. 国は宇宙開発に投入する資金を他のことに使うべきだ。 [Yes / No]

Vocabulary ＿＿に適する青色の単語の意味を枠内から選び、記号で答えましょう。

1. surface of the moon   月の＿＿
2. human existence   人間の＿＿
3. past century   過ぎ去った＿＿
4. space exploration   宇宙＿＿
5. develop rockets   ロケットを＿＿
6. impressive achievement   ＿＿偉業
7. sample of dust   ＿＿の標本
8. the Earth's atmosphere   地球の＿＿
9. remarkable success   ＿＿成功
10. current change   ＿＿変化

| a. 今起こっている | b. 存在 | c. 世紀 | d. 表面 | e. 微粒子 |
| f. 感動的な | g. 開発する | h. 素晴らしい | i. 探索 | j. 大気 |

While Reading 本文をパートごとに読み、あとの問題に答えましょう。

Part 1

 1960年代から始まる宇宙開発と日本の関わりについて英文を読んでみよう。

1. "That's one small step for a man, / one giant leap for mankind." /

2. These were the words / spoken by Neil Armstrong / in 1969 / as he became the first person / to set foot on the surface / of the moon. / The significance of this achievement / cannot be overstated. / It is amazing to think / that in the 200,000 years of *Homo sapiens*' existence, / we have managed to walk / on another world / for the first time / only in the past half century. / This suggests / that we are still at the very beginning of space exploration, / and Japan is playing an important role. /

3. Japan has sent / almost as many people into space as Germany, / and only the Unites States and Russia / surpass their numbers. / However, / it is unmanned missions / where Japan has mostly excelled. /

4. Japan is one of a few countries / that has been developing rockets / and launching satellites / since the space age began / in the 1960s. / Among the many space projects / that Japan has carried out, / its most impressive achievement so far / has probably been the *Hayabusa* mission. /

Notes　leap「飛躍」　Neil Armstrong「ニール・アームストロング（アポロ11号の船長）」
set foot on ...「…に足を踏み入れる」　Homo sapiens「ホモサピエンス、人類」
manage to *do*「どうにか…する」　play a role「役割を果たす」　surpass「…をしのぐ」
unmanned「無人の」　launch「打ち上げる」　satellite「人工衛星」

Exercises

(1) / の区切りごとに意味をとって本文を読み、次の英語の説明と合う単語を探して、提示の語頭に続けて答えましょう。ただし、名詞は単数形を、動詞は原形を書きましょう。

1. the importance, or the meaning of something　　　　　(s　　　　　　　　)
2. to say something in a way that makes it seem more important　(o　　　　　　　　)
3. to do something much better than most people　　　　(e　　　　　　　　)

(2) 本文の内容に合うように次の質問に英語で答えましょう。

1. Is it in the 20th century that the first person walked on the moon?
   — _____

2. Do we have a rather long history of space exploration?
   — _____

3. Is Japan playing an important role in space exploration?
   — _____

(3) 空所を補って、本文の内容に関する次の会話を完成させましょう。

Saki:　アームストロング船長が月面で言った「これは ¹._____
　　　　だが、人類にとっては ²._____ だ」って言葉は有名だわ。

Kenta:　半世紀も前のことだけど、人類が誕生してからの20万年を思えばまだ
　　　　³._____ ばかりだね。

Saki:　宇宙に行った人の数では日本はドイツとほぼ同じで、⁴._____
　　　　に次いで第3位だとは知らなかったわ。

Kenta:　それに日本は宇宙時代の始まりからずっと ⁵._____
　　　　_____してきた。宇宙開発に関わってきた数少ない国の一つなんだね。

Saki:　数々の日本のプロジェクトの中でも、いちばん感銘を受けたのはやっぱり「はやぶさ」よね。

Thinking Time!

 p.123 の My Opinion Note A を使って、自分の立場や意見を答えよう。

Part 2

「はやぶさ」やその他の日本のプロジェクトについて、さらに英文を読んでみよう。

5 *Hayabusa* was launched in May 2003 and two and a half years later it successfully landed on an asteroid, about the same size as a big stadium, nearby the orbit of Mars. The probe stayed for only about half an hour, and it collected samples of dust. It finally returned to the Earth in June 2010. Although it burned up as soon as it entered the Earth's atmosphere, a small capsule containing the dust arrived intact in Australia. This remarkable success has helped scientists learn more about how the solar system formed and how life began.

6 Presently, Japan has several space projects running. One of these is *Akatsuki*, a space probe that is currently orbiting Venus, the bright star that is often seen in the evening and early morning. *Akatsuki* is sending back information about Venus's atmosphere, which is terribly hot and thick. Such research can be helpful in understanding the current changes occurring in our own atmosphere. Japan is now planning a mission to the Martian moon, Phobos, hoping to bring back samples from the surface. However, they don't expect to find aliens, just microbes at the very best. As for our own moon, Japanese probes will be arriving soon.

Notes asteroid「小惑星」 the same ... as ～「～と同じくらいの…」 orbit「軌道」 Mars「火星」
probe「探査機」 capsule「カプセル」 intact「無傷の」 solar system「太陽系」 Venus「金星」
Phobos「フォボス（火星の第1衛星）」 microbe「微生物」 at the very best「（よくても）せいぜい」

Exercises

(4) 本文を、意味の区切りごとに / を入れて読みましょう。

(5) 空所を補って、「はやぶさ」に関する情報を完成させましょう。

2003年5月：1._____。

2005年：2._____の近くの3._____くらいの大きさの4._____に着陸。
　　　　滞在時間は5._____。
　　　　6._____を採集。

2010年6月：地球に7._____。8._____に9._____を入れたカプセルが帰着。

→　科学への貢献：10._____、および
　　　　　　　　11._____を知る手がかりとなった。

(6) 「あかつき」について、次のキーワードをすべて日本語にして用いて説明しましょう。

[space probe　　Venus　　information　　atmosphere　　current changes]

_____
_____
_____

Listening Comprehension

ケンタとアビーの宇宙開発に関する会話を音声で聴き、次の英文が会話の内容に合っていればT (True)、合っていなければF (False) を [　] に記入しましょう。

[　] 1. Kenta respects NASA's achievements in space exploration.

[　] 2. Abbie says Japan has been training a lot of astronauts.

[　] 3. Kenta hopes that *Akatsuki* will bring useful information back to the Earth.

Thinking Time!

 p.123 の My Opinion Note B を使って、自分の立場や意見を答えよう。

After Reading

日本語に合うように英文を完成させましょう。なお、下線部に相当する表現は提示しています。

1. グラウンドに足を踏み入れないで。雨でぬかるんでいるよ。 [set foot on]

   (　　　　) (　　　　) (　　　　) (　　　　) the ground.

   It's muddy after (　　　　) (　　　　).

2. 私はどうにか期日に課題を提出した。 [manage to *do*]

   I (　　　　) (　　　　) (　　　　) the (　　　　)

   (　　　　) the due date.

3. その広告は売り上げを上げるのに重要な役割を果たした。 [play a role]

   The (　　　　) (　　　　) an (　　　　) (　　　　) in

   increasing the (　　　　).

4. 私はあなたのものと同じ腕時計を持っている。 [the same ... as 〜]

   I have the (　　　　) (　　　　) (　　　　) (　　　　).

5. この前の試験では私はせいぜい平均点だろう。 [at the very best]

   I will get an (　　　　) mark (　　　　) (　　　　)

   (　　　　) (　　　　) in the (　　　　) (　　　　).

My Opinion Note

Student ID: _____   Name: _____

Unit 1 Japanese Cultural Invasion

A 次の英文を読んで、自分の立場や意見に当てはまるほうを○で囲みましょう。

1. I like reading manga. [Yes / No]
2. I sometimes buy manga. [Yes / No]
3. I know manga and anime are having an impact outside of Japan. [Yes / No]
4. I have seen an anime movie at the theater. [Yes / No]
5. All age groups can enjoy manga and anime. [Agree / Disagree]

B 次の英文を読んで、自分の立場や意見に当てはまるほうを○で囲みましょう。

1. I know about the Cool Japan campaign. [Yes / No]
2. Japan should protect and promote traditional culture more. [Agree / Disagree]
3. I know that Hello Kitty is popular outside of Japan. [Yes / No]
4. I tend to believe that a product with the name "Hokkaido" is fresh and good. [Yes / No]
5. I believe that Japanese culture will make the world more interesting. [Yes / No]

Write Your Opinion

次の質問に対する自分の答えや考えを書きましょう。

> What aspect of Japanese culture would you like to introduce to the world? Why are you proud of it?
>
> あなたならどのような日本文化を世界に紹介したいと思いますか。また、なぜそれを誇りに思うのですか。

Your Opinion

My Opinion Note

Student ID: _____ Name: _____

Unit 2 Emoji: From Japan to the World

A 次の英文を読んで、自分の立場や意見に当てはまるほうを○で囲みましょう。

1. I use emoji a lot in my messages. [Yes / No]
2. Without emoji, it would be more difficult to express my feelings. [Yes / No]
3. Emoji are a new kind of alphabet. [Agree / Disagree]
4. Emoji are universal, and everyone should immediately be able to understand them. [Agree / Disagree]
5. I'm proud of emoji being created in Japan. [Yes / No]

B 次の英文を読んで、自分の立場や意見に当てはまるほうを○で囲みましょう。

1. I know the word "emoji" is used outside of Japan, too. [Yes / No]
2. Kanji are like pictures, and much more attractive than English alphabet. [Agree / Disagree]
3. I knew the news that the Oxford Dictionary named "Face with tears of joy" its word of the year. [Yes / No]
4. I often use the smiling face emoji. [Yes / No]
5. Emoji will become more and more commonplace in the world. [Agree / Disagree]

Write Your Opinion

次の質問に対する自分の答えや考えを書きましょう。

> How do you use emoji in your messages? How are they useful in them?
>
> あなたはメッセージの中で絵文字をどのように利用していますか。また、それはどのように役立っていますか。

Your Opinion

_____

_____

_____

_____

_____

_____

_____

_____

_____

_____

My Opinion Note

Student ID: _____   Name: _____

Unit 3 Tokyo 2020: Chance for a New Beginning

A 次の英文を読んで、自分の立場や意見に当てはまるほうを○で囲みましょう。

1. I have seen some pictures or videos of the 1964 Tokyo Olympics.　[Yes / No]

2. It is a good idea to hold the Olympics in a country that has something to show the world.　[Agree / Disagree]

3. I am happy that Tokyo has been chosen as a host country of the 2020 Olympics.　[Yes / No]

4. Hosting the Olympics will bring Japan a lot of prestige.　[Agree / Disagree]

5. Japan has already recovered from the Great East Japan Earthquake.　[Agree / Disagree]

B 次の英文を読んで、自分の立場や意見に当てはまるほうを○で囲みましょう。

1. I'm worrying about the cost of the 2020 Tokyo Olympics.　[Yes / No]

2. The money spent on the Olympics should be used for earthquake recovery efforts.　[Agree / Disagree]

3. We didn't have to completely rebuild the National Olympic Stadium.　[Agree / Disagree]

4. Generally, Japanese people are looking forward to the 2020 Tokyo Olympics.　[Agree / Disagree]

5. The 2020 Tokyo Olympics will be a big success.　[Agree / Disagree]

Write Your Opinion

次の質問に対する自分の答えや考えを書きましょう。

> Are you for or against hosting the Olympic Games? Give two reasons why.
>
> あなたはオリンピックを主催することに賛成ですか、それとも反対ですか。その理由を2つ述べて意見を書きましょう。

Your Opinion

_____
_____
_____
_____
_____
_____
_____
_____
_____
_____

My Opinion Note

Student ID: _____   Name: _____

Unit 4　Pet Obsession

A　次の英文を読んで、自分の立場や意見に当てはまるほうを○で囲みましょう。

1. It is ridiculous to serve a dog a breakfast of minced Kobe beef.　　[Agree / Disagree]

2. It is ridiculous to dress a dog in a designer outfit.　　[Agree / Disagree]

3. I was surprised at the number of pets, which is larger than that of people under 15.　　[Yes / No]

4. When someone feels lonely, it is a good idea to have a pet as a companion.　　[Agree / Disagree]

5. People don't have to buy expensive pets because there are lots of stray dogs and cats.　　[Agree / Disagree]

B　次の英文を読んで、自分の立場や意見に当てはまるほうを○で囲みましょう。

1. I know about the Shogun, Tokugawa Tsunayoshi, who protected dogs.　　[Yes / No]

2. I know the story of Hachiko, the dog that continued to wait for his master in front of Shibuya Station.　　[Yes / No]

3. Owners must not abandon their pets for any reason.　　[Agree / Disagree]

4. Putting down abandoned pets cannot be helped.　　[Agree / Disagree]

5. I would be willing to be a new owner if a pet really needed me.　　[Yes / No]

Write Your Opinion

次の質問に対する自分の答えや考えを書きましょう。

> Would you like to have a pet? Why or why not?
> あなたはペットを飼いたいと思いますか。また、それはなぜですか。

Your Opinion

My Opinion Note

Student ID: _____   Name: _____

Unit 5   Silver Japan

A 次の英文を読んで、自分の立場や意見に当てはまるほうを○で囲みましょう。

1. I am well aware of Japan's aging society.　　　　　　　　　　[Yes / No]

2. Japan should accept more immigrants.　　　　　　　　　　　[Agree / Disagree]

3. Japanese society treats elderly people well.　　　　　　　　　[Agree / Disagree]

4. I know the story that in the past grandma was carried into the mountains and left to die.　　　　　　　　　　　　　　[Yes / No]

5. Elderly people should spend their pension more to help the Japanese economy.　　　　　　　　　　　　　　　　　[Agree / Disagree]

B 次の英文を読んで、自分の立場や意見に当てはまるほうを○で囲みましょう。

1. It is good that an aging society will give the younger generation more job opportunities.　　　　　　　　　　　[Agree / Disagree]

2. I would like to go into the health care profession in the future.　　　　　　　　　　　　　　　　　　　　[Yes / No / Not sure]

3. Less severe crowding will bring the younger generation a more comfortable and enjoyable life.　　　　　　　　　[Agree / Disagree]

4. The Japanese government should not raise taxes; instead, it should look for another way to manage pensions.　　　　[Agree / Disagree]

5. An aging society has more disadvantages than advantages.　　[Agree / Disagree]

Write Your Opinion

次の質問に対する自分の答えや考えを書きましょう。

> What kind of life do you think silver Japan will bring to you?
> 高齢化社会はどのような生活をあなたにもたらすと思いますか。

Your Opinion

My Opinion Note

Student ID: _____   Name: _____

Unit 6   Changing Gender Roles

A   次の英文を読んで、自分の立場や意見に当てはまるほうを○で囲みましょう。

1. I would be surprised if I saw a female sushi chef behind a counter.   [Yes / No]

2. I have taken a taxi whose driver is female.   [Yes / No]

3. It feels strange to see a man cooking in the kitchen.   [Yes / No]

4. I believe men and women should keep their traditional roles in family life.   [Yes / No]

5. Husbands and wives should share house chores equally if they are a working couple.   [Agree / Disagree]

B   次の英文を読んで、自分の立場や意見に当てはまるほうを○で囲みましょう。

1. Women are too delicate to handle the stress of being a pilot.   [Agree / Disagree]

2. Women are not strong enough to be members of the Self-Defense Forces.   [Agree / Disagree]

3. We should not blame busy fathers for working late.   [Agree / Disagree]

4. I can't understand people whose priority is their work.   [Yes / No]

5. Gender role reversals will happen more and more in Japan.   [Agree / Disagree]

Write Your Opinion

次の質問に対する自分の答えや考えを書きましょう。

> Do you think one gender should be preferred on any occupation? If you said yes, explain your reasons. If you said no, can you think of any exceptions?
>
> どの職業においても男性か女性のどちらか一方だけが望ましいという考えは当然だと思いますか。そう思う場合は理由を、そう思わない場合は例外を答えましょう。

Your Opinion

My Opinion Note

Student ID: _____   Name: _____

Unit 7   Maternity Harassment

A 次の英文を読んで、自分の立場や意見に当てはまるほうを○で囲みましょう。

1. I would give my seat to a pregnant woman on train. [Yes / No]

2. I would not be willing to do extra work to help a pregnant coworker. [Yes / No]

3. I understand why employees make cruel remarks if they have to work harder because of their pregnant coworker. [Yes / No]

4. A pregnant woman should not expect any special treatment because having a baby is a personal matter. [Agree / Disagree]

5. I would like (my wife) to continue working after having a baby. [Yes / No]

B 次の英文を読んで、自分の立場や意見に当てはまるほうを○で囲みましょう。

1. New mothers should not be demoted under any circumstances. [Agree / Disagree]

2. I know about labor laws that protect working pregnant women. [Yes / No]

3. The therapist in Hiroshima should not have sued the hospital. [Agree / Disagree]

4. If a pregnant woman sues her company, she should not be afraid of criticism. [Agree / Disagree]

5. Women should have the freedom to continue working while pregnant, as well as after they give birth. [Agree / Disagree]

Write Your Opinion

次の質問に対する自分の答えや考えを書きましょう。

> Do you think Japanese society needs more women's labor power or not? Why or why not?
>
> 日本社会はもっと女性の労働力が必要だと思いますか。また、なぜそう思うのですか。

Your Opinion

My Opinion Note

Student ID: _____   Name: _____

Unit 8 Digital Youth: The Connected Generation

A 次の英文を読んで、自分の立場や意見に当てはまるほうを○で囲みましょう。

1. I feel my cell phone is part of my body. [Yes / No]
2. I almost always keep my cell phone on. [Yes / No]
3. When a new message comes in, I usually check it immediately. [Yes / No]
4. Social networks with friends are useful to seek an identity. [Agree / Disagree]
5. I get a lot of information, such as music and photos, through my cell phone. [Yes / No]

B 次の英文を読んで、自分の立場や意見に当てはまるほうを○で囲みましょう。

1. Young people often ignore their studies because of their phones. [Agree / Disagree]
2. I sometimes feel depressed about seeing my friends always having a good time. [Yes / No]
3. I sometimes have problems with my eyes and neck when I stare down at my cell phone for hours. [Yes / No]
4. Parents complain about their children in every generation. [Agree / Disagree]
5. Generally, there are more advantages than disadvantages with cell phones. [Agree / Disagree]

Write Your Opinion

次の質問に対する自分の答えや考えを書きましょう。

> To what extent do you think you are connected or unconnected now? Give a couple of examples.
>
> あなたは現在どの程度、携帯を使っていますか。いくつか例を挙げて説明しましょう。

Your Opinion

My Opinion Note

Student ID: _____ Name: _____

Unit 9 Japan's Peaceful Poor

A 次の英文を読んで、自分の立場や意見に当てはまるほうを○で囲みましょう。

1. I cannot imagine life without electricity. [Yes / No]

2. It is cruel that power companies cut off electricity when poor people cannot pay their bills. [Agree / Disagree]

3. I feel sorry for Hiroshi as he lost his full-time job due to his company's restructuring. [Yes / No]

4. Everyone should be prepared for the risk of losing his or her job. [Agree / Disagree]

5. I hope I can work for the same company all my life. [Yes / No]

B 次の英文を読んで、自分の立場や意見に当てはまるほうを○で囲みましょう。

1. There is a big difference between the rich and the poor in Japan. [Agree / Disagree]

2. I would like to be a celebrity and dine at a luxury restaurant in Ginza. [Yes / No]

3. It is surprising that almost 40 percent of Japanese workers are casual or part-time workers. [Agree / Disagree]

4. Patience (*gaman*) is very important in life, and it is good that poor people accept their poverty. [Agree / Disagree]

5. I have bought discounted food on its expiry date. [Yes / No]

Write Your Opinion

次の質問に対する自分の答えや考えを書きましょう。

> Why do you think poor people in Japan are generally more peaceful compared to the poor overseas?
>
> なぜ日本の貧しい人々は海外の貧しい人々と比べて、概して穏やかなのだと思いますか。

Your Opinion

My Opinion Note

Student ID: _____ Name: _____

Unit 10   The Idol-Making Machine

A　次の英文を読んで、自分の立場や意見に当てはまるほうを○で囲みましょう。

1. Idols must be young and cute, or cool.   [Agree / Disagree]
2. Idols need not be talented.   [Agree / Disagree]
3. If a talent agency recruited me, I would refuse to be an idol.   [Yes / No]
4. An untalented idol should not play an important role in movies.   [Agree / Disagree]
5. An image of innocence is very important to be an idol.   [Agree / Disagree]

B　次の英文を読んで、自分の立場や意見に当てはまるほうを○で囲みましょう。

1. Generally, the songs idols sing sound almost the same.   [Agree / Disagree]
2. It is not surprising that talent agencies are just interested in making money.   [Agree / Disagree]
3. Talent agencies spend much money on future idols, so idols should not complain if their agency controls their lives.   [Agree / Disagree]
4. Idols should not have boyfriends or girlfriends.   [Agree / Disagree]
5. There is nothing wrong with the way Japanese idols are made.   [Agree / Disagree]

Write Your Opinion

次の質問に対する自分の答えや考えを書きましょう。

> The Japanese system of making idols is distinctive. Do you agree with the system? Why or why not?
>
> 日本のアイドルの作り方は独特です。その方法に賛成ですか。また、それはなぜですか。

Your Opinion

_____
_____
_____
_____
_____
_____
_____
_____
_____
_____
_____
_____

My Opinion Note

Student ID: _____   Name: _____

Unit 11 Japanese Hospitality: Second to None

A 次の英文を読んで、自分の立場や意見に当てはまるほうを○で囲みましょう。

1. The language salespeople use with their customers is very important. [Agree / Disagree]

2. If a salesperson treated me impolitely, I would complain about it to the manager. [Yes / No]

3. It feels good to hear that Japanese hospitality is special. [Yes / No]

4. If I were a clerk and a customer asked me where a product was, I would take the person right to it. [Yes / No]

5. I would welcome visitors to Japan with special hospitality. [Yes / No]

B 次の英文を読んで、自分の立場や意見に当てはまるほうを○で囲みましょう。

1. Japanese companies should expand their way of hospitality to the world. [Agree / Disagree]

2. It would probably be difficult to train people outside of Japan in a Japanese way. [Agree / Disagree]

3. The service provider should expect nothing from the customer. [Agree / Disagree]

4. Tipping is a good way to express "thank you" to the service provider. [Agree / Disagree]

5. Japanese hospitality will probably change in the future. [Agree / Disagree]

Write Your Opinion

次の質問に対する自分の答えや考えを書きましょう。

> Are you proud of Japanese hospitality? Or do you have any disagreement? Give a couple of reasons for your position.
>
> あなたは日本のおもてなしを誇りに思いますか。もしくは異論がありますか。理由をいくつか挙げてあなたの意見を述べましょう。

Your Opinion

___
___
___
___
___
___
___
___
___
___

My Opinion Note

Student ID: _____   Name: _____

Unit 12 Shrinking Cities: Returning the Countryside to Nature

A 次の英文を読んで、自分の立場や意見に当てはまるほうを○で囲みましょう。

1. I knew the news about Yubari's decreasing population. [Yes / No]

2. Yubari melons are extraordinary, so the government should protect the farmers. [Agree / Disagree]

3. Tokyo is an attractive city with a lot of activities. [Agree / Disagree]

4. I understand why young people would want to leave their shrinking hometowns. [Yes / No]

5. The government should find some way to attract people to Yubari as the town has lots of nature and quality products. [Agree / Disagree]

B 次の英文を読んで、自分の立場や意見に当てはまるほうを○で囲みましょう。

1. I often eat bread or pasta instead of rice. [Yes / No]

2. I don't want a job in which my hands get dirty. [Yes / No]

3. Working behind a desk for hours sounds boring. [Agree / Disagree]

4. Rural areas may have a chance to become wealthy. [Agree / Disagree]

5. Some towns are shrinking and some cities are overcrowded. This is quite normal and nothing can be done about it. [Agree / Disagree]

Write Your Opinion

次の質問に対する自分の答えや考えを書きましょう。

> Where would you like to work? In a big city? Or in a rural village? Why?
>
> あなたは大都市と地方の村ではどちらで働きたいですか。また、それはなぜですか。

Your Opinion

My Opinion Note

Student ID: _____ Name: _____

Unit 13 Student Power: The New Youth Movement

A 次の英文を読んで、自分の立場や意見に当てはまるほうを○で囲みましょう。

1. I have read or heard the news about the student movements in the late 1960s. [Yes / No]

2. Students need not be interested in politics. [Agree / Disagree]

3. Some people are political, and others are non-political. We cannot say which side is better. [Agree / Disagree]

4. I know the controversy over the interpretation of the constitution. [Yes / No]

5. I often talk about politics with my friends. [Yes / No]

B 次の英文を読んで、自分の立場や意見に当てはまるほうを○で囲みましょう。

1. It is good that the voting age has been lowered to 18 years. [Agree / Disagree]

2. Eighteen-year-olds should be recognized as adults. [Agree / Disagree]

3. Young people will not be able to generate significant change in society. [Agree / Disagree]

4. Students should learn a lot about politics at high school. [Agree / Disagree]

5. It is wrong for students to behave as they did in 1960s and 1970s because we should not be violent in any situation. [Agree / Disagree]

Write Your Opinion

次の質問に対する自分の答えや考えを書きましょう。

> How would you like Japanese society to be?
> あなたは日本の社会がどのようであればよいと思いますか。

Your Opinion

My Opinion Note

Student ID: _____ Name: _____

Unit 14 Japan in Space: Leaping to New Frontiers

A 次の英文を読んで、自分の立場や意見に当てはまるほうを○で囲みましょう。

1. I know the famous words Neil Armstrong spoke on the moon. [Yes / No]

2. I don't understand why it is significant for human beings to be on the moon. [Yes / No]

3. It is surprising that more Japanese and Germans have gone into space than any other country except the USA and Russia. [Agree / Disagree]

4. I'm proud that Japan has excelled in unmanned missions. [Yes / No]

5. I have heard the news about *Hayabusa*. [Yes / No]

B 次の英文を読んで、自分の立場や意見に当てはまるほうを○で囲みましょう。

1. It is surprising that just dust of an asteroid can tell a lot of important facts to us. [Agree / Disagree]

2. I would like to know how life began. [Yes / No]

3. It is important to understand the current changes occurring in our own atmosphere. [Agree / Disagree]

4. Advancing technology and spending money on space exploration are important to our future. [Agree / Disagree]

5. There must be life elsewhere in the universe. [Agree / Disagree]

Write Your Opinion

次の質問に対する自分の答えや考えを書きましょう。

> Do you support Japan's contribution to exploring space? Why or why not?
>
> あなたは日本の宇宙探索への貢献を支持しますか。また、それはなぜですか。

Your Opinion

Word List

このリストには、本書の While Reading 本文（Part 1 と 2）で使われている重要な語句や表現とその初出ページを収録しています。ただし、固有名詞は除外しています。

※ Vocabulary で取り上げている語句は青字で示し、NOTES で取り上げている語句はページ番号のあとに N を付けています。

A

a day	62N
a dozen	80
abandon	28N, 34
accelerate	46N
acting ability	70N
activism	88N
addicted	58
adorn	16
adulthood	88N
affect	40
allow	52
approach	86N
archipelago	82N
as ... as possible	20N
as a result	34N
as for	80N
associate with	14N
asteroid	94N
at all	50N
at least	22N
at the very best	94N
atmosphere	94
attachment	34
attention	34
attract	82
avoid *doing*	46N

B

be aware of	38N
be driven by	38N
be familiar with	34N
be known for	32N
be related to	64N
be similar to	14N
be unlikely to *do*	58N
because of	50N
behavior	46
believe in	86N
beside	22
bill	62
blockbuster	14N
bother to *do*	88N
bring about	88N
bronze statue	34N
bullying	50N
business	74N

C

cane	80N
capsule	94N
cause	86N
celebration	50
century	92
challenge	28N
Chinese characters	22N
chore	44N
coal worker	82N
coincidence	22
colleague	50
come to an end	86N
come to *do*	50N
commonplace	22
companionship	32
competition	26
complain	28
concept	76
concern	58
construction	62
consumption tax	40N
continue *doing*	52N
contract	70
controversy	28
convey	14
creative	56
criticism	52
crowding	40
cruel	50
current	94

D

decline	82N
decrease/decreasing	82
dedicated to	16N
defeat	26
deficit	28
delicate	46
demand	82
demote	52N
depend on	82N
depressed	58
description	44N
designer outfit	32N
destroy	70
develop	92
device	22
diaper	80N
diet	82
dine	64
distinctive	14
domestically	82N
due to	38N
dust	94

E

effectively	20
effort	82
either A or B	70N

election	88	hosting country	26N	**M**	
electricity	62			made up of	22N
enforce	52N	**I**		maintain	82
entertainment field	68N	icon	16N	make a living	62N
envy	70	ignore	38	make sense	46N
era	26N	illustrate	74	manage to *do*	92N
ever-present	56N	immediately	20	march	86
examine	76	impressive	92	Mars	94N
exceedingly	32	in fact	50N	maternity leave	52N
exclusive to	44N	in one sense	58N	may have + 過去分詞	58N
exercise	58	in return for	76N	meaningless	70
existence	92	in the meantime	62N	media coverage	88N
expand	40	in the middle of	56N	microbe	94N
expiry	64	in the worst case	52N	middle-class	64N
exploration	92	incoming	58	minced beef	32N
export	16	industry	68	mold	44N
extreme	38	initial	28	monochrome	20N
		innocence	68	morning sickness	50N
F		innovative	82N	mother-to-be	50N
fame	70N	inspire	20		
fantasy	70N	intact	94N	**N**	
fictional	32	interaction	76	national median salary	62N
financial	40	interpretation of the constitution	86N	no longer	64N
fire	52			no matter what	22N
flippant	70N	irregular	62	normally	50N
focus	74	it goes without saying that	68N	not all	70N
focus on	14N				
forecast	20	it is only recently that	16N	**O**	
full of	16N			occupy	28
		L		once	74N
G		labor law	52N	opportunity/opportunities	40
gain	14	lack	50		
generate	88	launch	92N	optimism	28N
give birth	52N	lawyer	44	orbit	94N
given	22N	lead to	64N	organically	82N
go beyond	76N	leap	92N	outskirt	82N
graciously	74	legal	52		
grim	38	less	64N	**P**	
		lifespan	38N	pager	20N
H		lock	70N	patience	64
handle	46	look like	26N	pension	40N
have + O + 動詞の原形	70N	lower	88N	personal identity	56N
have no problem *doing*	40N	loyalty	32	phenomenon	20N
head out to	82N	luxuries	28N	Phobos	94N
Homo sapiens	92N	luxury	64	physical	58
hostel	62N			platform	56N

play a role — 92N	retail company — 76N	this is why — 76N
polite — 74	retractable — 28N	threaten — 52
political — 88	reveal — 52N	three-dimensional — 14N
politician — 88	reversal — 44	thus — 28N, 56N
post — 58	reward — 76	tip — 64N
potential — 70	rice farming — 82N	too ~ to — 32N
pour — 44	rural — 82	tough — 70N
poverty line — 62N		towards — 44
poverty rate — 64N	**S**	traditional — 16
pregnant — 50N	satellite — 92N	trap — 46
prestige — 26	search — 16N	treatment — 50
pre-teenage — 70N	seek — 56	trivial — 68
prevent — 64	Self-Defense Forces — 46N	
previous — 88	set foot on — 92N	**U**
priority — 46	share with — 56N	unemployment rate — 40N
prison — 86	shelter — 34	universal — 20
probe — 94N	significant — 14	unlike — 26N
product — 16N, 74	silver walker — 80N	unmanned — 92N
profession — 40	slice — 44	up to — 88N
profit — 70	so (that) + S + (can) V — 56N	
promote — 16N	solar system — 94N	**V**
proposal — 86	span — 14N	Venus — 94N
propose — 20	specific — 68	vibration — 58N
protection — 34	spend money on — 28N	violent — 86
provider — 76	spread — 16	vivid — 14
publicize — 52N	stare — 58	vote — 88
purchasing — 38N	statistics — 38N	voting — 38N
put down — 34N	struggle — 81	
	such as — 28N	**W**
Q	sue — 52N	wealth — 64
quality — 16	Supreme Court — 52N	where to *do* — 74N
	surface — 92	whether — 56N
R	surpass — 92N	would rather *do* — 82N
realistic — 32		
rebound — 26N	**T**	
recovery — 28	take over — 82N	
refined — 76N	take responsibility — 44N	
relatively — 86N	talent agency — 70N	
remain — 64N	tea ceremony — 16N	
remarkable — 94	tens of thousands of — 82N	
remarkably — 26	the fact is — 44N	
replace — 40	the median age — 80N	
reputation — 82	the same ... as — 94N	
resemblance — 22N	there is no need to *do* — 70N	
respectively — 14N	there is still much to *do* — 52N	
result in — 28N	third-world country — 26N	

クラス用音声 CD 有り（別売）

Portraits of Japan
—Voicing Opinions on a Changing Society
日本を知り、そして世界を知り、そして考える

2017 年 1 月 20 日　初版発行
2024 年 4 月 10 日　第 7 刷

著　者　Paul Stapleton、上村淳子
発行者　松村達生
発行所　センゲージ ラーニング株式会社
　　　　〒102-0073　東京都千代田区九段北 1-11-11　第 2 フナトビル 5 階
　　　　電　話　03-3511-4392
　　　　FAX　03-3511-4391
　　　　e-mail: eltjapan@cengage.com
　　　　copyright © 2017 センゲージ ラーニング株式会社

装　　丁　森村直美
組　　版　MAT（一ノ瀬湯夫）
本文イラスト　湊　敦子
印刷・製本　株式会社ムレコミュニケーションズ

ISBN 978-4-86312-312-0

もし落丁、乱丁、その他不良品がありましたら、お取り替えいたします。
本書の全部または一部を無断で複写（コピー）することは、著作権法上での例外を除き、禁じられていますのでご注意ください。